Vietnam's
Christians

I have been waiting for this book. What a tantalizing mystery Vietnam is. The long heritage of the people. The trauma of war. Today's hot economy. The continuing legacy of Marxist persecution. And, through it all, the church of Jesus Christ. What does it mean to be a Christian in this land? How have believers inside and outside the country offered wise witness, service, and advocacy? This book tells the story in solid context. Details never before revealed come to light.

Miriam Adeney, PhD
Associate Professor of World Christian Studies, Seattle Pacific University
Teaching Fellow, Regent College
Author, *Kingdom without Borders*

My friend and missionary colleague, Reg Reimer, is a passionate advocate for the cause of religious freedom. I consider Reg to be the most knowledgeable person on the church in Vietnam, and I am grateful he took time to write this moving and informative book. When Roman Catholic clergy and laity were martyred for their faith centuries ago, "the gates of hell did not prevail against it." When Protestant missionaries, pastors, and believers were imprisoned or killed during the Vietnam War, the light of the gospel continued to shine. After Vietnam's unification in 1975, the church multiplied, despite restrictions and persecution. That is the encouraging story of this book. I pray that in years to come, the Lord will use the testimonies and experiences of our Vietnamese brothers and sisters to strengthen the church in the free world and to spread the gospel to all the corners of the earth!

Johan Companjen
President Emeritus, Open Doors International

Vietnam's Christians: A Century of Growth in Adversity is a must-read for anyone wishing to understand how the gospel of Jesus Christ entered Vietnam. Reg Reimer skillfully weaves personal experiences into the text to offer depth and texture to the turbulent history and exponential growth of the church. This book is a welcome reminder of the great work the Lord is doing in Vietnam.

Corey Odden
Chief Executive Officer, The Voice of the Martyrs (Canada)

My fascination with Vietnam began as a teenager after hearing Reg Reimer speak. Since then I have followed Reg's intriguing journey with great interest. Reg has distinguished himself as a missionary, a mentor, and advocate for all things Vietnam. In these pages he captures the powerful story of a resilient people of God who through a blend of physical courage and spiritual depth have thrived in the midst of huge challenges. I was clearly reminded that God often chooses some of the darkest and most challenging hours in history to do some of His greatest work.

Charles A. Cook, PhD
Professor of Global Studies and Mission,
Ambrose University College & Seminary
Executive Director, Jaffray Centre for Global Initiatives
Chair, Global Mission Roundtable (EFC), Calgary, Alberta, Canada

At last the secret is out! For too long the story of the astonishing growth of the Vietnamese church has lain unknown, underreported, or even ignored. Yet it is one of modern Christianity's most encouraging triumphs. Reg Reimer has done the worldwide body of Christ a huge favour in giving us the first definitive account of the progress of the gospel in Vietnam. Comprehensive and scholarly, nuanced and inspirational, yet told with the care and love that comes from one who was not only a scholarly observer *of* the story, but a vital participant *in* the story. This book deserves to become a modern missions classic and will challenge and change all who read it.

Ron Boyd-MacMillan, PhD
Chief Strategy Officer, Open Doors International and
Author of *Faith that Endures: The Essential Guide to the Persecuted Church!*

I call the author of this book my "older brother." Reg Reimer, a lifelong missionary to my native Vietnam, helped launch my international ministry in a moving event described in these pages and has been a great encourager to me ever since. I know of no better source to find such a moving summary of the heroic missionary beginnings and of the explosive growth of churches after missionaries left Vietnam than this remarkable book.

Phan Thi Kim Phuc, the "Napalm Girl"
President, Kim Foundation International and
renowned worldwide speaker

I am very pleased with the publication of Reg Reimer's short and precise telling of the expansion of the Protestant movement in Vietnam during its first one hundred years. This is the only such publication which includes the tumultuous last thirty-five years. Reimer is a keen observer of the social, political, and religious conditions in Vietnam. He skillfully weaves his own missionary experience into the story. As a professor I highly recommend this short history as a valuable sourcebook for those interested in the growth of the church in the Global South, as a textbook for seminarians, and as a guidebook for church planters.

Rev. Duc X. Nguyen, PhD
President, Vietnam World Christian Fellowship, Inc.

I was mesmerized from the first page. This book will challenge your definitions of commitment, suffering, and devotion to the cause of Christ. Even I, as a Vietnamese pastor, did not know the extent to which Vietnamese Christians before me risked everything to follow Christ, some paying the ultimate price. If you are up for a faith challenge I invite you to read here stories of great courage and true sacrifice. You will meet Vietnamese believers and foreign missionaries faithfully witnessing and serving Christ under extreme conditions and tremendous difficulties over many years—simply sold out for Christ. In my opinion, all Vietnamese Christians owe missionary Reg Reimer a debt of gratitude for this record of our story.

John Nguyen, DMin
President, Vietnamese National Baptist Fellowship, USA

This book is *exactly* what you would expect from the world's foremost expert on evangelicalism in Vietnam: inspired, intelligent, and incisive. Erudite and eyewitness, Professor Reimer tells a powerful and personal story that also provides perspective. Comprehensive and contextual, this account will serve both students and scholars, in seminaries and Southeast Asian studies. As he links familiar history with faithful presence, Reimer's presentation of the past will help Vietnam frame the future: a future where all Vietnamese have the freedom to choose or change faith.

Chris Seiple, PhD
President, Institute for Global Engagement

For many of us, Reg Reimer is the person with the best read on the situation of the church in Vietnam over the past thirty years, and so I am very pleased to see the publication of this book. Reg provides his readers with a passionate and insightful overview of the state of the church, particularly the suffering church, of Vietnam. His writing is compelling: well-documented accounts of the growth of the church, probing analyses of the issues that shaped the life of the church through and after the war of the 1960s, and carefully chosen narratives of the lives and experience of specific individuals. It is all a testimony to the grace of God and the perseverance of the church through a particularly difficult chapter.

Gordon T. Smith, PhD
President, reSource Leadership International

Reg Reimer simply refused to give up. Pushed out of his country of choice, he and Donna continued to serve the Vietnamese in diaspora everywhere. When I met Reg it wasn't long until I learned of his heart for Vietnam and its people. He had become fluent in their language and deeply understanding of their life and ways. All of that comes together in this marvelous book of insight and challenge. Significantly, alongside this invaluable chronicle of history and personal memories, a vibrant Christian community grows in Vietnam today. Surely a legacy of his vision, love, and deep resolve.

Brian C. Stiller, PhD
President Emeritus, Tyndale University College and Seminary
Toronto, Canada

Nobody is more qualified than Reg Reimer to write this seminal book on the history of the church in Vietnam. Conceived out of history, birthed in his own years of ministry on-site, and followed by decades as a watcher and advocate, Reg will move you to gratitude, to worship, to mission.

William D. Taylor, PhD
Senior Mentor, WEC Mission Commission
World Evangelical Alliance

The history of the church in Vietnam is the saga of courageous followers of Christ who often experienced the reality of His presence under very difficult circumstances. The examples of faithful Vietnamese Christians and the brave missionaries who brought the gospel to them will inspire and challenge all who read this book. I highly recommend it.

Arie Verduijn, President
Alliance World Fellowship, Veenendaal, Netherlands

I represent many, many Christians here in Vietnam when I sincerely thank Professor Reimer for telling our story to the world. I hope it will soon be translated into our language. Please let this book help you pray for us.

A church leader in Vietnam

Vietnam's Christians

A Century of Growth in Adversity

REG REIMER

WILLIAM CAREY
LIBRARY

Vietnam's Christians: A Century of Growth in Adversity
Copyright © 2011 by Reg Reimer

Published by William Carey Library
1605 E. Elizabeth St.
Pasadena, CA 91104 | www.missionbooks.org

Kelley K. Wolfe, editor
Brad Koenig, copyeditor
Josie Leung, graphic designer
Rose Lee-Norman, indexer

Photos contributed by Kim Phuc, Dr. David Thompson, and Danh Phuoc Thanh.

William Carey Library is a ministry of the
U.S. Center for World Mission
Pasadena, CA | www.uscwm.org

16 15 14 13 12   6 5 4 3 2 BP1500

Printed in the United States of America

Library of Congress Cataloging-in-Publication Data
Reimer, Reg.
  Vietnam's Christians : a century of growth in adversity / by Reg Reimer.
     p. cm.
  Includes bibliographical references and index.
  ISBN 978-0-87808-304-6
  1. Vietnam--Church history--20th century. 2. Protestant churches--Vietnam--History--20th century. 3. Vietnam--Church history--21st century. 4. Protestant churches--Vietnam--History--21st century. I. Title.
  BR1187.R45 2011
  275.97--dc22

                                        2011012042

To the Reverend Doan Van Mieng,
my Vietnamese "Father,"
and longtime leader of the Evangelical Church Of Vietnam—South
who called me to "Raise our voice in the outside world;
we cannot speak for ourselves."

To the many men and women I know
who have "done time for Jesus" in Vietnam.

To the many believers who have been and still are
joyful and faithful in adversity.
"The world is not worthy."

Contents

Religious suffering is, at one and the same time, the expression of real suffering and a protest against real suffering. Religion is the sigh of the oppressed creature, the heart of a heartless world, and the soul of soulless conditions. It is the opium of the people. The abolition of religion as the illusory happiness of the people is the demand for their real happiness.

Karl Marx in "Contribution to the Critique of
Hegel's Philosophy of Right" from *Marx/Engels Collected Works*

No one with a good conscience and who respects the truth is incapable of realizing that the State of Vietnam always cherishes and creates favorable conditions for all its citizens to exercise their freedom of religion. The State of Vietnam has never obstructed any religious activities.

Hanoi Army Daily, September 12, 1999

The President [Nguyen Minh Triet of Vietnam] pointed out that the Vietnamese State has now and before always respected and ensured the citizen's right to freedom of belief and considered religious followers an integral part of the national unity.

Vietnam New Agency, December 12, 2009
(on occasion of President Triet's visit with Pope Benedict)

Lies written in ink can never disguise facts written blood.

Lu Xun

There were those who, under torture, refused to give in and go free, preferring something better, resurrection. Others braved abuse and whips, and, yes, chains and dungeons. We have stories of those who were stoned, sawed in two, murdered in cold blood, stories of vagrants wandering the earth in animal skins, homeless, friendless, powerless—the world didn't deserve them!—making their way as best they could on the cruel edges of the world.

(Hebrews 11:35b–38, *The Message*)

Foreword

The story of the church in Vietnam is one of the greatest in history. For four centuries, the Catholic church sought to live faithfully, enduring fierce persecution, and 130,000 martyrs, and now has some eight million followers, among the largest churches in Asia. Their history, as recounted here, is astounding and almost unbelievable.

The Protestant church, though younger, in its century of life has endured similar hardship, and has born tremendous fruit. Especially since 1975, much of the growth in Vietnam has been in the evangelical churches. As Reg Reimer recounts, in that year there were about 160,000 evangelical believers. Now there are some 1.4 million, a growth of 900 percent.

Throughout history, Christianity has tended to thrive among the marginalized, and in Vietnam much of the spread of the gospel has been among the ethnic minorities of the Central Highlands and the Northwest Mountainous Region. The former are those often called "Montagnards," simply French for "mountain people," and the latter also includes many diverse groups, the largest of which is the Hmong. These people have seen church growth in the hundreds of thousands, and now some peoples are majority Christian. And the church also grows steadily among ethnic Vietnamese.

As in other places in the contemporary world, much of the growth of the church has taken place after the major missionary presence had ended. This is certainly no criticism of the faithful missionaries who, as carefully described here, devoted their lives, even unto death, to serve the Vietnamese. It is, instead, a dramatic testimony to their work: they planted and nurtured carefully and well, and the seed has sprung up and born fruit after they were forced to go.

Despite faithfulness and victory through persecution, the Vietnamese church story is comparatively little known in the West. Perhaps this is due to lingering Western guilt over the American role in the Vietnam War. But, if so, it is thoroughly misplaced in so far as the Vietnamese community of believers is concerned. While they seek and cherish all contact with and encouragement from fellow believers, including those missions that have continued to offer brave and careful support, this is a thoroughly indigenous, strong, vibrant, independent church.

This is the first book-length study that recounts the history of the Vietnamese church since the 1975 reunification under communism. It covers much more than this period, but it is the most detailed and synoptic survey of the amazing events of the last thirty-five years.

There are few, if any, more qualified to write this than Reg Reimer. One of my most cherished memories of him was in Brussels following an international meeting on work with the persecuted church. Reg found, of course, a Vietnamese restaurant close to the Grand Place and greeted the waiters, and then the owner, and then their families, in fluent Vietnamese. His joy in meeting them was matched by theirs in finding a Westerner who spoke their language and loved their people, culture, and, need I say, their food.

Reg came to this deep-seated knowledge and love by serving as a missionary in Vietnam from 1966 to 1975, and then for years giving support to the church from postings in nearby countries. Since then he has managed to visit regularly, often discreetly, with leaders to support and record the life of the church. He has been a witness. As he recounts, in 1980, a senior church leader appealed to him, "Raise our voice in the outside world: we cannot speak for ourselves."

My own work is documenting religious freedom and religious persecution around the world. In reporting on the persecution of the church in Vietnam, I, and other human rights groups, know that there is no more careful, current, and informed witness than Reg Reimer. I have been constantly amazed by what he knows and how he knows it.

The year 2011 is the centennial of Protestantism in Vietnam. It is a fitting time for all Christians and, indeed, for all people of goodwill, to learn of the history of Vietnamese Christians. It is a story of drama and suffering, and of inspiration, hope and victory. There is no better place to learn it than in *Vietnam's Christians: A Century of Growth in Adversity*.

Paul Marshall

Senior Fellow, Hudson Institute Center for Religious Freedom
Author of over twenty books, many on religious freedom

Preface

Some time ago my wife and I visited a missionary colleague in northern Thailand. Her wooden home was backed against a steep hill. Looking through a window at eye level we could see bamboo shoots emerging from the ground. Our hostess told us that during the rainy season she sometimes measured six inches (fifteen cm) of growth in a single day! It is with this same vitality that the church in Vietnam has grown.

A colleague and I recently visited the Vietnam Center at Texas Tech University in Lubbock, Texas. I knew well its reputation as the largest collection of Vietnam resources in the world. Yet I was surprised to see a veritable warehouse of thousands of books and huge volumes of other materials, mostly spawned by the American period in Vietnam in the 1960s and 1970s. A Vietnam researcher's dream! On the other hand, the young researcher who showed us around was quite intrigued to meet me. He said their vast collection had very little on the century-old Protestant movement in Vietnam and wondered if I could contribute.

If there is a gap in that famous collection, there is an even greater one in Christian, particularly mission, literature. Though a number of books were published during the American–Vietnam War and some personal missionary memoirs since, this small volume is the first summary of the Vietnam Protestant story. Far too many Westerners' ideas of Vietnam have been shaped by the war, which often eclipsed equally compelling and much longer stories. Importantly too, this year marks the beginning of the second century of Protestant presence in Vietnam.

Respected colleagues and mission leaders convinced me that it would be good stewardship to capture my unique experiences and knowledge of the Protestant movement in Vietnam as equity forward for churches there and for the mission community. So the incentives to write mounted.

The stories here are fascinating enough, I hope, to capture popular Christian readers as they learn of significant developments that God is shaping in the world's thirteenth largest nation. For those who are being called to participate in creatively supporting churches and mission in Vietnam, this book will outline the foundations and the significant superstructure already built. To these, I urge, go first as learners. Vietnam is far, far past missionary ground zero and, indeed, can be a wise teacher. Specialists will here encounter significant past and present missiological issues in the Vietnam context, and scholars may discern interesting subjects for much-needed further research.

I hope as well to inform the many thousands of Vietnamese in diaspora about God's work in the country from which they have long been separated. To all readers I offer some windows and resources to further discover not only Christian history but also wider cultural and political insights on Vietnam.

It will be helpful to consider what I have written here in its global context. While I focus on the particularities of Vietnam in recent decades, the significant growth of Christianity amid suffering and hardship is, in many ways, the story of the entire Global South.

The rapid rise of Christianity in the Global South, well known to those of us in the mission community but few others, has been both academically and popularly documented by Philip Jenkins. His books, *The Next Christendom: The Rise of Global Christianity* (2002) and *The New Faces of Christianity: Believing the Bible in the Global South* (2006) are doing much to counter Western ignorance about a gigantic historical phenomenon. His work powerfully challenges the false assumption of many that religion, particularly Christianity, is in decline in the world. Indeed, Jenkins suggests humankind's primary allegiances in the twenty-first century may well be religious, replacing earlier ideological ones.

Vietnam demonstrates common characteristics of Christianity in the Global South. One is a very literal reading of the Bible. Unlike many

Western Christians whose "Enlightenment" history and experience has dimmed their sight, Southern Christians are at home in the supernatural worldview of the New Testament. People constantly battered by oppression, poverty, disease, and violence can see these as demonic, literally, and actively seek divine deliverance. Hence the appeal and popularity of the most rapidly growing brand of Christianity in the world—the Pentecostal/charismatic variety—which hearkens back to early Christianity and which emphasizes the demonstrable power of God.

Leaders of this kind of Christianity, like the reformers of five centuries ago, take their authority directly from the Bible and often eschew hierarchy. What results is certainly vital, but often individualistic and messy. In Vietnam, as elsewhere, these characteristics have given birth to many small denominations, where previously there were very few.

Christianity in the Global South also provides what my seminary professor Donald McGavran described as "social lift." Christian conversion leads directly to better personal and communal values and mores, which in turn lead to family stability and prosperity. These can, if allowed, also contribute significantly to a more just, fair, and prosperous society. I say, "if allowed." In Vietnam, Communist Party theorists in 1990 proposed the potentially breakthrough idea that religion could contribute cultural and moral values even in a socialist society. Regrettably, orthodox Marxist beliefs about religion still stall the accommodation of this breakthrough idea. In Vietnam and elsewhere, the dance between Christians and Communists remains very jerky.

Readers may be shocked at some description of the persecution of Christians in Vietnam. Though communism has now fallen behind radical Islam as an engine of Christian oppression and persecution, it remains harsh at worst and ambivalent at best in relation to Christianity. But, I venture to say, of the remaining five Communist countries, always-pragmatic Vietnam is probably the one with the most hope for positive change.

Suffering and persecution come as no surprise to followers of Jesus Christ. Our Lord promised the same to all who came after him. From the first apostles and the early church, Christians throughout history have experienced severe adversity. In Vietnam, religious oppression, persecution, and martyrdom accompanied the rapid growth of Christianity a full three centuries before communism.

In March 2011 the British branch of the Vatican-approved organization, Aid to the Church in Need, released a report called "Persecuted and Forgotten?" It found that 75 percent of religious persecution in the world today is against Christians. It also says that in two-thirds of the countries where persecution occurs, the situation has worsened. The report concludes, "For millions of Christians around the world persecution, violence, discrimination, and suffering are a way of life as they live out their faith" (Pontifex 2011).

Not long before his mysterious "resignation," I was introduced to the brilliant Archbishop of Hanoi, Ngo Quang Kiet. Two Protestant leaders who had worked with the Catholics on Bible publication and distribution took me to visit him in his historic residence on Nha Chung Street. I will never forget the breathtaking painting hanging on the wall of the large reception room, depicting a multitude of Catholic martyrs. You will read briefly about some of them here.

By way of introducing me, one of my colleagues told the archbishop that I had taught church growth in the Protestant seminary in Nhatrang before 1975. The atmosphere felt a bit tense, so I joked, "Yes, but I had to leave Vietnam before the church really grew!"

The archbishop quickly responded, "So you are like Jesus; it is better that you leave!" (John 16:7). The tension melted, and we moved quickly to a deeper level of fellowship.

My comment referred to the fact that in the thirty-five years since the reunification of Vietnam under communism, with the absence of foreign missionaries and in spite of great adversity, Protestant churches have grown by 900 percent! To that largely untold story, which covers the last third of the first Protestant century, I dedicate the last half of this book.

I make no pretense of being a disinterested observer. I am a full and enthusiastic participant and, I hope, a reflective one, in the ongoing Vietnam Christian drama.

As a witness to this drama and a friend of its key leaders, I humbly relate some of the courageous stories that they themselves cannot yet tell. Someday, soon I trust, they will be able to share fuller and richer versions.

Reg Reimer
Yverin Muse
Glacier, Washington
Ash Wednesday, 2011

Acknowledgments

The situation in Vietnam regrettably remains such that I should not name and publicly thank the many indigenous sisters and brothers who have long taken risks to help me know and understand their story. Some other colleagues, both inside and outside of Vietnam—missionaries, journalists, diplomats, and others—might also be "inconvenienced" if I named them. You know who you are. Thank you. Thank you.

Jean Gainor, the most able personal assistant I ever had, was the most persistent among many who urged me to write this story. It was Glenn Penner, who left us too soon, who finally pushed me over the start line.

I am forever grateful to my greatest and longest encourager in life and ministry, my wife LaDonna. She did so much to help me create space for this labor.

I thank my friend and mentor, Bill Taylor, who introduced me to William Carey Library. It has been a pleasure to work with the skilled staff there as they helped me birth my work into this book.

Timeline

early 1600s	Roman Catholic missions established in Vietnam
1890s	First Protestant missionary forays into Vietnam
1911	Missionaries of the Christian and Missionary Alliance establish permanent mission station at Danang
1921	First full-time Bible school for training pastors opened in Danang
1926	Entire Protestant Bible translated and published
1929	Indigenous Vietnam Evangelical Church established
1936	John Sung revival
1941–1945	Japanese occupation and a great famine. Most missionaries depart but a few are interned
1945–1954	War of Independence against the French
1954	Geneva Accords divide Vietnam north and south at the seventeenth parallel
early 1960s	Other evangelical missions begin to arrive in the south
1964–1973	The American–Vietnam War
1971	The Nhatrang revival
1975	The "Fall of Saigon" or "Liberation Day" on April 30. Vietnam united under communism. Total number of evangelicals 162,000
1975–1985	The "Dark Decade" or the first ten years under communism for the South
1978–1983	The Tran Cao Van revival
1986	Vietnam launches *doi moi* (renovation of its economic system)
1988	House church movement begins

2004–2005   Vietnam introduces "new religion legislation" intended to
                  move from "decrees" toward more religious freedom
2004–2006   Vietnam placed on list of worst religious liberty offenders
                  by the US and then removed
2011   Centennial celebration of the Protestant movement in
                  Vietnam. Total number of evangelicals rises to estimated
                  1.4 million

Introduction

In the thirty-five years since a divided Vietnam was united under communism in 1975, the number of evangelical believers has grown from some 160,000 to 1.4 million—nearly 900 percent![1] This remarkable growth, under a regime always suspicious of and often hostile toward Christianity, is a fascinating and instructive story.

Through many twists, turns, and setbacks, and in spite of much gratuitous suffering by God's people in Vietnam, a faithful God grew His church and fostered faithfulness in His people.

The perspective from which I write this story is very much shaped by my own experience. I went as a missionary to Vietnam with my wife and two small children in December of 1966, just as the Vietnam War was sharply escalating. Just over a year later, in the infamous 1968 Tet Offensive, Communist soldiers murdered six fellow missionaries in the Central Highlands town of Banmethuot. Three of us missionaries buried three of them in the soil where they died. The high cost of serving Christ was indelibly impressed on my heart in those dark days.

With a missionary community of about two hundred people in twenty organizations, we continued to serve alongside courageous Vietnamese Christians, preaching the good news of Jesus Christ and responding in His love to the massive human need generated by war, until the fall of South Vietnam in April of 1975.

Then, from a posting in nearby Thailand, we responded to the needs of refugees fleeing the newly Communist nations of Cambodia, Laos, and

---

1   A complete presentation of religious and particularly Christian statistics for Vietnam may be found in *Operation World* (Mandryk 2010, 882–886).

Vietnam. From the survivors who escaped vicious pirates during treacherous sea voyages in small boats, and from others who braved arduous overland escapes, we learned the grim realities of living under the Communist regimes and their special hostility toward Christian believers.

In 1980, in the middle of Vietnam's first "Dark Decade" under communism, I managed quite improbably to visit fellow believers there. In a secret meeting with top church leaders, I learned firsthand of the incredible suffering of God's people. When I asked what I should do, the senior leader responded without hesitation, "Raise our voice in the outside world; we cannot speak for ourselves." That became a clarion call for me.

In the thirty years since, that calling became a main vocation. It has involved numerous trips to Vietnam, an untold number of meetings with hard-pressed and persecuted Christians, and the translation of many hundreds of pages of official government documents, some of them top-secret. It is still "not convenient," as one would say in Vietnamese, to share all the ways I have "raised the voice" of Vietnamese Christians. But it is that experience and record from which I draw to tell you their stories in these pages. The research I did for my seminary dissertation in 1972, entitled *The Protestant Movement in Vietnam: Church Growth in Peace and War*, provides the earlier history.

The year 2011 marks the centennial of Protestantism in Vietnam. In this short book I will highlight the growth and obstacles encountered by evangelical Protestant churches during its first one hundred years. Of necessity it will be a selective telling, and one that can only begin to explain the layered complexities of Vietnam and its history.

It will be instructive to first consider the Roman Catholic Church in Vietnam to provide a context for my focus on evangelical Protestant experience. With four centuries of history and some eight million followers, it is second in size in all of Asia only to the Catholic Church in the Philippines. The fierce persecution of early Catholic missionaries and their Vietnamese converts is an unbelievable and little-known chapter in church history.

Since 1975, for a full third of its first hundred years, Protestant Christianity has grown and indeed flourished in a Vietnam under communism. This is the first published attempt to summarize what has happened during these tumultuous years.

The very "explosion" of evangelical Protestant Christianity, as some government documents have called it, and the multiplicity of outside efforts to support churches in Vietnam make it impossible to be exhaustive. But we can discern the streams, movements, and leaders and recognize that God is at work, building His kingdom. We also see clearly that the best efforts of a hostile ideology cannot frustrate this grand and eternal enterprise.

A Large and Prominent Country

Vietnam, now the thirteenth most populous country in the world with eighty-six million people, was vaulted into the spotlight of world attention in the 1960s as America's war there escalated. Vietnam became at once a center of controversy, a focus of anguish, and an object of pity. For the first time in history, highly developed global communications made it possible for millions around the world to watch man's inhumanity to man on evening television shows, virtually as it was happening. And it tore people's souls.

It is well known that the Vietnam War cost the Americans more than fifty-eight thousand lives, untold drain on the national treasury, and a serious loss of international self-confidence. It came to define a generation of Americans and still casts its long shadow over American foreign policy. The war spawned countless serious studies, self-analyses, novels, and movies.

What is not so well known is that the cost of the "American War," as Vietnamese call it, was many times greater for Vietnam, and has been much less told.

But it is the kingdom of God subtext, or should I say primary text, to all this that concerns us here. God is at work in the affairs of this world, whether we recognize it or not. We can certainly find His fingerprints in Vietnam!

Criticizing Vietnam

It is widely considered not "cool" to criticize Vietnam, which seems to occupy a unique place in Western thinking. While human rights groups continue to document that Communist Vietnam is a very oppressive regime, the country seems to get off rather easily. Courageous Vietnamese dissidents often receive scant support in their efforts to ameliorate the effects of one of the world's last Communist dictatorships.

Perhaps it is collective Western guilt over the perils of American hubris in Vietnam where terrible things happened forty years ago. Also, with a booming economy and tourist sector, and with the state's complete control of local media and clever manipulation of international news learned as a war strategy, Vietnam somehow manages to limit international scrutiny and criticism.

However, in Vietnam those who dare challenge one-party rule—the poorest people and the religious believers—still experience harsh discrimination and the dictator's heavy boot. We cannot allow Vietnam's past suffering at the hands of outsiders to hide the truth about those who suffer now at the hands of their own government. We will concentrate on the lot of Protestant believers. Vietnam is improving, but still has a long way to go.

A Mini-guide

Though they make up only 13 percent of Vietnam's people, ethnic minorities make up well over half of the Protestants in Vietnam, and so they will take up considerable space in our story. They reside in Vietnam's Central Highlands (CH), also called the Western Highlands, and the Northwest Mountainous Region (NMR).

Vietnam government publications always speak of fifty-four ethnic groups in Vietnam. Wycliffe linguists calculate that, linguistically defined, the number actually approaches one hundred.

The CH border Cambodia to the west, north of Ho Chi Minh City (HCMC), Vietnam's commercial capital.[2] The CH area is the traditional home of several dozen ethnic minorities or tribes. They belong to two separate language families called Mon Khmer and Malayo Polynesian. Collectively the CH tribal groups are called "Montagnards," French for "Mountain People." More than 400,000 Montagnards have become Christians since the gospel first came to them in the 1930s.

---

2   The name for Saigon was officially changed to Ho Chi Minh City in 1976. The city is often, however, referred to by its original name, which in Vietnamese as in English is three syllables shorter than the new. The names are used interchangeably in this book without political implications.

Among the main groups with large numbers of Christians are the Ede, Jarai, Koho, Stieng, and Bahnar.

The NMR lies at the top of Vietnam, bordering China on the north and Laos on the west. It is also the traditional home of several dozen ethnic minorities, the largest of which is the Hmong. As many as 350,000 ethnic minority people, chiefly Hmong, have become Christians in just the last two decades. These new Hmong Christians are zealously sharing the gospel with other, heretofore un-reached ethnic groups such as the San Chi.

The ethnic Vietnamese traditionally populated the coastal lowlands, but land pressure has also pushed them into the CH, where they now outnumber Montagnards, and also into the NMR.

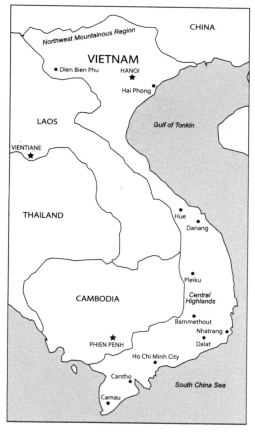

CHAPTER 1

Contradictions

An Amazing Event

Vietnam is a land where complete contradictions are often found side by side. Two events in the space of a December 2009 fortnight provide a snapshot of the situation of Vietnam's Christians.

On December 11, 2009, history was made in Communist Vietnam. Some forty thousand people gathered in a hastily constructed venue in Ho Chi Minh City to celebrate Christmas and hear a gospel message—an event of unprecedented magnitude and significance in Vietnam. A popular Vietnamese Christian website and other reports indicated that up to eight thousand people responded to the gospel message with a desire to follow Christ.

Though they had given verbal approval months earlier, authorities refused to grant the necessary written permission for the event. In fact, they tried urgently to talk leaders out of going ahead, promising future concessions if they would cancel the event. But the organizers stood up and persisted. They had prepared for this moment with weeks of focused prayer by hundreds of people. They warned the government of negative consequences in Vietnam and abroad if the long-planned event was not allowed to proceed.

Just forty-eight hours before the scheduled start of the event, officials finally gave their permission—but for only three thousand people. This gave organizers less than two days to turn a vacant field into something that would accommodate a stadium-sized crowd. They had to bring in ample electricity, construct a giant stage, and set up the sound and lighting. They dared exceed their permission and set up twenty thousand chairs. Hundreds of students responded to text messages, sacrificing classes to help with last-minute preparations and join in the celebration. Organizers also rented hundreds of busses to bring Christians and their non-Christian friends from provinces near the city. At least two thousand people had to be turned away.

House church Christians, who rarely gather in large numbers, found the giant worship service thrilling beyond their imagination. They joined the choir of a thousand singers in joyful praise and singing. The climax came when thousands of the non-Christian friends they had brought indicated a desire to follow Christ. Pastor Duong Thanh (Samuel) Lam of the Assemblies of God house churches preached with divine anointing. People who responded to his gospel invitation poured to the front of the stage "like a waterfall."[3] All this in Communist Vietnam!

A Counterpoint Reality Check

At the very same time, quite another story was unfolding in the northwest mountains of Vietnam. Dien Bien province has long had the reputation as the worst spot in a bad area—a law unto itself when it comes to Christians. Its governing officials seem intent on keeping that reputation.

In November 2009 an itinerant evangelist led ten Hmong families to faith in a commune of Dien Bien Dong district. One of them, Mr. Pao Xyooj, believed in Christ after he was healed of a long-standing disease as a result of the evangelist's prayer. Local officials immediately pounced on these families, threatening them with large fines and great harm should they persist in their new belief. Seven families recanted but three did not.

On December 1, police incited a large number of non-Christian villagers to beat and stone the three families who refused to go back on their new faith. Mr. Pao and his wife were left cut and badly bruised, but still held fast. Their appeal for help reached friends abroad.

On December 15, police took Mr. and Mrs. Pao to her parents and family. The police incited Mrs. Pao's parents to apply strong social pressure by threatening to ostracize the couple completely. This is a very powerful force in a communal society. The police added that if Mr. Pao would not recant they would beat him to death, take all of his possessions, and leave his wife a homeless widow and his children orphans. Later, on the phone, a distraught

---

3   A Vietnamese language website at www.hoithanh.com regularly posts interesting information about the activities of Protestant churches in Vietnam.

Mr. Pao told a missionary abroad, "I folded, I signed the form. I believe in my heart, but the officials do not allow us to follow Christ." His wife could be heard sobbing in the background.

Within a few days this story reached foreign offices and some Vietnamese embassies in London, Washington, and Ottawa. But Vietnam did nothing quickly to confront its officials for seriously violating its own laws and breaking its international promises. It rarely does.

Mr. Pao and family remained firm in their faith in spite of his forced signature to the contrary. The price they paid was high. On February 2, 2010, hostile family and community officials confiscated the family's entire year's supply of rice paddy and all their household utensils. Three weeks later authorities dismantled the Pao family house, and on March 19 the family was expelled and fled into the forest.

These contrasting events symbolize the religious freedom situation in Vietnam. When unregistered house churches united and stood up to authorities accustomed to getting their way by threats, the authorities backed down. The much-blessed Christmas event happened in spite of the authorities. Though they tried hard to stop it and appeared to hold all the cards, the authorities failed. The power of prayer and Christian unity prevailed!

Meanwhile, in the high mountains, far away from the glare of a large city and without international presence, new ethnic-minority believers were subjected to excruciating social pressure, physical abuse by mobs, and death threats from officials to get them to recant. And some new believers did, if only on paper. Without opportunity for pastoral counsel and with little Bible knowledge, they wrestled with the question, "Will Christ forgive me for signing the form promising to go back to worshiping my ancestors?"

This goes on in a country that declares to the world it guarantees full religious freedom for all its citizens and has never done anything to hinder religious practice!

The Road Ahead

The thirty-five years under communism have taught Vietnamese Christians valuable lessons. The most important is God's keeping power for those who endure what He allows them to experience. Christian leaders, recognizing that persecution often strengthens and sometimes contributes to growing the church, want most of all to be found faithful.

However, they legitimately desire to be respected as full citizens in their country and to contribute to their nation. They are weary of being suspected, marginalized, discriminated against, and hounded by their government. They boldly ask fellow Christians around the world to pray for them and to advocate internationally to hold their government accountable to its promises. They credit advocates and foreign governments with the progress in religious freedom that has been made, and they request that we not let up now.

Vietnam's churches are building creative ministry partnerships with Christians and organizations around the world. These will serve Vietnam best if they work together.

Vietnamese Christians have much to teach Christians in more peaceful lands. In their extremity they have come to understand better than many, the awesome power of the God of the Bible. God has shown Himself strong for His people. Signs and wonders often accompany bold evangelism.

Believers in Vietnam are not only bold but optimistic. They trust in Him who said, "I will build my church, and the gates of Hades will not overcome it" (Matt 16:18).

Which Way Vietnam?

Journalists from major Western news agencies have lived and worked in Vietnam since the mid-1980s. A number of them, whom I came to know, helpfully published religious liberty abuses. Several also wrote insightful reflections following their departure from Vietnam which was not always at a time of their own choosing. Four books give particularly good snapshots of the Vietnam the authors experienced. They also deal with the big questions on the minds of many. For example: "Will economic liberalization and betterment lead to political and other freedoms?" Their conclusion is usually, "Not soon."

Murray Hiebert, an American who had worked in South Vietnam as a Mennonite volunteer, represented the respected *Far Eastern Economic Review*[4] in Hanoi from the mid-1980s until the mid-1990s. Based on his private notes, which he

---

4   *The Far Eastern Economic Review,* noted for fearless reporting on economic and political matters in Asia since WWII, regrettably ceased publication in 2009.

was able to smuggle out with considerable difficulty, he published *Chasing the Tigers: A Portrait of the New Vietnam* (Hiebert 1996). It turned out to be a fairly accurate prediction of the amazing economic growth Communist Vietnam would experience following its gradual abandonment of Marxist economic principles.

British journalist Robert Templer, who worked in Vietnam for Agency-Press France, published *Shadows and Wind: A View of Modern Vietnam* (Templer 1998). His stay in Vietnam was cut short when, as was the case for some other too-probing journalists, his visa was not renewed. Templer captures well the complex social dynamics of Vietnam in the 1990s, including the huge inequities Vietnam's emerging state capitalism was producing.

David Lamb served as a *United Press International* and *Los Angeles Times* war correspondent in the late 1960s. Believed to be the only war correspondent to do so, Lamb returned to live in Hanoi from 1997 to 2001. The outcome was *Vietnam Now: A Reporter Returns* (Lamb 2002). Like many who sojourn there, Lamb admits to being smitten by the country and people of Vietnam. Some consider his excellent account of Vietnam during his time there a bit too uncritical of the regime.

The latest is a book by journalist Bill Hayton who reported from Hanoi for the BBC in 2006 and 2007. *Vietnam: Rising Dragon* (Hayton 2010b) focuses on how today's Vietnam really works. It is an excellent primer for anyone considering living and working in Vietnam. It peels back some of the many layers of Vietnam's bureaucratic decision making which begins and ends with Party. He describes how Vietnam values tradition but is ultimately pragmatic. Hayton deftly sees through the official propaganda with what he observes in the daily lives of real people. Many outsiders who have lived in Vietnam for a lot longer than Hayton have understood much less.

In a web posting entitled "The Limits to Political Activity in Vietnam" (Hayton 2010a), he accurately summarizes what other perceptive insiders have observed. He states that one-party political control in Vietnam, including complete dominance of all media, is only half of the story. Party dominance is in constant tension with one of the most dynamic and aspiring societies on the planet, ever willing to push the envelope. In Vietnamese this is called *pha rao* or "breaking fences." It enables the people to raise their standard of living and do many things not particularly favored by the Party in spite of the many fences around them—so long as they do not challenge the supremacy of the Party.

The Party maintains ultimate control and has no intentions of giving up the "leading role" given it by Article 4 of Vietnam's constitution. As for well-meaning, outside attempts to influence Vietnam toward more freedom, Hayton observes:

> Millions of dollars and euros have been spent by international donors promoting legal reform, political pluralism, and better journalism. But throughout the entire reform process, the Communist Party has remained several steps ahead of the donors . . . International aid and investment have not brought multi-party democracy to Vietnam: instead it has made one-party rule more efficient and effective. That is the way the Party likes it. Life is getting better for the vast majority of Vietnam's people, and as long as that continues, that is the way things will stay. (ibid.)

CHAPTER 2

Vietnamese Culture and Religion

What was the religious context into which Christian missionaries and the gospel first entered?

Still today, if one were to ask a rural peasant farmer in Vietnam whether he had a religion, he would likely say, "No, I only worship my ancestors," meaning he does not consider himself a member of an organized religion such as Catholicism or Buddhism. But if religion is defined as any belief or practice used by people to explain their relationship with the visible and invisible worlds around them, the ancestor worshiper is, of course, a religious person. Vietnamese are indeed a very religious people.

A great many misconceptions concerning Vietnamese religion exist in popular writings. A major one concerns the dominance of Buddhism. Being of the Mahayana or "broad way" Buddhist stream, the Buddhism of Vietnam does not have the predominance over people's lives as does Theravada Buddhism in neighboring Cambodia, Laos, Burma, or Thailand. The Buddhism of Vietnam is intertwined with animism and also considerably influenced by Taoism and Confucianism. Some Vietnamese say they follow a combination of the "three religions."

Buddhism is popularly said to be Vietnam's main religion. But the number of Vietnamese who actually identify themselves as Buddhists is much disputed. The Government Bureau of Religious Affairs (GBRA) has published the number as ten million, or 12 percent of the population.[5] The 2009 government census figures, which have lower figures than the GBRA for all religions (Central Population and Housing Census Steering Committee 2009,

---

5   From a Vietnamese-language, internal government *Protestant Training Manual* printed in 2010.

Annex 3), says Vietnam has only 6.8 million Buddhists, or 6.6 percent of the population. Some Buddhist leaders would claim up to thirty million or more.

Underlying Animism

The acknowledged authority on Vietnamese religion was an amazing Catholic priest named Father Leopold Cadiere. He was also an authority on Vietnamese history, art, and language. He served in Vietnam for sixty-three years, from 1882–1945, when he died in a Viet Minh prison.[6]

The underlying web of Vietnamese religion is pervasive animism. In great detail Cadiere describes the intricacies of this web as being as complex as a multilayered tropical forest (Cadiere 1929, 275). Religious feelings dominate all aspects of Vietnamese society in a powerful way, from lofty state rituals accompanying the installation of an emperor to nodding to a stone believed to be infused with spiritual power. It includes belief in geomancy, numerology, astrology, soothsayers, sorcerers, and in deifying local or national heroes. It would be a serious error to think that a generation or two of atheistic communism has done much to sweep this away. Much of this "superstition" is still widely practiced by the very Communist officials who denounce it as unscientific, to say nothing of ordinary people.

The veneration of ancestors is the most widely practiced religious ritual in all of Vietnam. This is a high form of animism which ascribes spiritual power to the spirits of departed family members.

Man was traditionally believed to have three souls and nine vital spirits. The souls of the deceased must be ritually honored on ancestral altars and sometimes at the tomb. Souls of those abandoned in death become errant and malevolent spirits. The rituals for honoring ancestors are among the most highly developed Vietnamese cultural institutions. A common term for these rituals is *tho cung*, meaning "worship and sacrifice." Casual observers often miss the importance of ancestor worship because it is a private ritual without a hierarchy beyond the family.

Cadiere concluded: "Such is the true picture seen not by the travelers who visit a few temples, nor the scholar who scrupulously delves into the liter-

---

6   Among his prolific writings in French was a three-volume masterpiece whose title, translated into English, is *Religious Beliefs and Practices of the Vietnamese* (Cadiere 1958).

ature related to the subject, but by those who have constantly under their eyes the manifestations of the religious life of the Annamese[7] nation" (ibid., 276).

Indigenous Religions

The religiosity of the Vietnamese can also be seen in the development of unique indigenous religions. Most well known among these is the Cao Dai religion, which dates from the 1920s. It is an outstanding example of syncretism that brings together often contradictory belief systems. In this case the founder, Ngo Van Chieu, who made communicating with the occult world through séances a key part of his religion, set about to deliberately syncretize various religions. A Cao Dai document candidly confirms this: "Caodaism is an amalgam, a synthesis of existing religions: Confucianism, Taoism, Buddhism, Christianity, and so forth. It also does not neglect animistic worship and the deification of heroes of Sino-Vietnamese history" (Gobron 1950, 159).

Cao Daists made saints of all the founders of religions they knew of— Jesus, Buddha, Confucius, Lao Tze, Brahma, Vishnu, Shiva, Mohammed, and more. Cao Dai's unique central temple in Tay Ninh, usually included on the tourist beat, mixes architecture of the cathedral, the mosque, and the oriental pagoda. Government figures put the total of Cao Dai adherents at 2.3 million, but Cao Dai leaders claim double that number.

Another indigenous religion, also primarily in Vietnam's Mekong Delta like Cao Daism, is called Hoa Hao. A reform Buddhist movement which dates to the 1930s, it developed a strong anti-Communist military wing and still arouses the distrust of the government. Government figures say there are 1.3 million Hoa Hao followers, but again, Hoa Hao leaders say it is more than double that. Both the Cao Dai and Hoa Hao religions have developed splits and "denominations." The government has recognized more than one Cao Dai group but only the one Hoa Hao group that it controls.

But now we move to the main story.

---

7   An earlier name for Vietnamese from the "Kingdom of Annam" and later the French Protectorate by the same name. It means "peaceful south."

CHAPTER 3

Alexandre de Rhodes and Early Roman Catholic Missions

> My sole ambition in my travels has been the glory of my good Captain Jesus Christ and the profit of the souls He conquers. I traveled neither for the sake of riches, nor for knowledge, nor to amuse myself. Through God's mercy, I sought no other pearls than those Jesus Christ glories to set in His diadem, no other knowledge than that which St. Paul preached . . . no other amusement beyond giving joy to the angels by converting not a few sinners. (de Rhodes 1966, xx)

The language may be quaint, but the object is clear. This early missionary was consumed with a passion to evangelize Vietnam. Alexandre de Rhodes was a luminary among the many European Catholic missionaries who, from 1615 onwards, sought to plant their church in Vietnam. His accomplishments between several expulsions from Vietnam are astounding.

While there are some references to Portuguese Catholic missionaries in the mid-sixteenth century, the Catholic faith was not established in Vietnam until 1615. That year, a number of Jesuit priests, expelled from Japan, established the first permanent mission near present-day Danang. Twelve years later Alexandre de Rhodes was chosen to establish a second mission in Tonkin, now northern Vietnam.

He learned the very difficult Vietnamese language within six months. Within three years he had recorded the baptism of 6,700 believers, including Vietnamese royalty! In his memoirs he remarked that "the faith was making too great strides . . . not to be opposed by the devil" (ibid., 70). Indeed, the dignity accorded ordinary people by Christianity directly challenged the hierarchical mandarin system. De Rhodes was expelled and went to Macau.

He returned five years later to the south, and after five years was again expelled, this time on penalty of death.

Father de Rhodes produced the remarkable *Eight Day Catechism* which became the basis for incorporating the many new converts into the church (Phan 1998). The amount of doctrine and story in this catechism far surpasses the modest content of modern formula evangelism! And, equally important, building on the work of some Portuguese predecessors, Father de Rhodes devised a brilliant and simple Romanization of Vietnamese ideography called *Quoc Ngu*, in which he published the *Eight Day Catechism* in parallel with Latin. This script replaced the Chinese-based ideography and was eventually adopted nationally. It became the vehicle for wide literacy and the introduction of outside ideas into Vietnam.

By 1660 the Catholic believers numbered in the hundreds of thousands. De Rhodes' journal and other writings make clear that the spiritual power of the priests in working miracles, healings, and exorcisms played a major part in this growth. It also attracted local shamans and Buddhist monks, who were confronted by God's superior power. Some of them brought all their followers for instruction and baptism. The European priests also believed that their native catechists had been invested with divine power to perform miracles, restore sight, and even raise the dead!

But the exploding church could not ordain priests. A papal decree had given Spain and Portugal sole authority to appoint bishops, who alone could ordain priests in newly discovered parts of the world. Father de Rhodes came to the rescue!

> Seeing I was the only priest who could preach, because the Father I was with didn't know the language, I decided to keep some Christians with me who were not married and who were filled with zeal and piety to help me in the conversion of souls . . . many offered their services but I chose those I thought most capable and started a seminary which succeeded so well we might say it's what kept us going. (ibid., 69)

These men became a functional lay clergy. This lay brotherhood built and kept the church going during many long periods when foreign missionary priests were forced to live underground or were expelled entirely.

Banished from Vietnam a final time in 1645, de Rhodes returned to Europe. His first priority was to find a way to have bishops appointed to Vietnam, where he had left a burgeoning church without a hierarchy that could ordain priests. He found a solution by inspiring the creation of a special office called an "apostolic vicar," or "missionary bishop," who had authority to ordain clergy even though he did not have a geographical diocese. Such bishops soon ordained clergy in Vietnam, thus regularizing church life.

Father de Rhodes also tirelessly promoted missions in Vietnam by speaking and writing. Out of these efforts came the Paris Missionary Society which mobilized diocesan priests and lay people in Europe to support missions. It became an important Catholic missionary sending agency in 1660.

The Heavy Persecution of Catholics

It should not be surprising that the rapidly growing Catholic Church attracted trouble. Vietnam's Confucian-oriented mandarins and rulers saw in Christianity a revolutionary religion whose principles of respect for human dignity and social justice threatened the established order. Further, a papal edict condemning all ceremonies connected with ancestor veneration in Asia in 1742 reversed the creative cultural adaptation of some early missionaries. Also, Vietnam's rulers feared that missionaries represented the vanguard of political aspiration in their European countrymen to colonize Vietnam.

And so, as early as the seventeenth century, missionaries were often expelled. Persecutions were unleashed against Christians from the seventeenth until the nineteenth centuries. In 1825 an edict outlawed "the perverse religion of the Europeans." A more inflammable edict in 1833 accused missionary priests of building churches "in order to seduce women and young girls . . . and to tear the eyes out of the dying." Unimaginably severe waves of persecution broke out between 1833 and 1840, from 1851 to 1863, and finally from 1868 to 1888.

Reimer (1972) summarizes the persecution of Vietnamese Christians. A little-known chapter in church history, it was the most protracted and cruelest action against Asian Christians in recent centuries. Christians were regularly deprived of their property, and their villages and churches were torched. Thousands of Christians were imprisoned for their faith and forced to wear around their neck a square wooden yoke called a *cangue*. This cangue became popularly known as the "cross of Indochina."

The bamboo cangues in this drawing of prisoners early in the twentieth century are much lighter than the ones used to punish Vietnamese Christians in the previous centuries. Those were made of a large flat hardwood board often  weighing from twenty to thirty pounds. The board consisted of two pieces which were closed around the Christians' necks and secured by locks.

Catholic believers were heavily pressured to recant. A simple test was used to determine the intensity of the religious loyalty of Christian believers. They could escape the worst punishment if they would but step on a wooden cross. Those who did were branded on one cheek with the words *ta dao* ("perverse religion") and the symbol of their district so they could not flee. Those who refused to step on the cross were further persuaded to give up their faith by beatings with split bamboo rods or by torture with hot coals and pincers. Christians were staked to the ground and exposed to the blazing tropical sun for long periods. They were put into cages and tormented with spears. They were thrown into human sewage, exposed to flesh-eating worms, or made to kneel on boards with protruding nails.

The great numbers who would not be dissuaded met a martyr's death. Catholic sources generally put the lowest total number at 130,000! Christians were strangled, sawn asunder, and tied together in long lines and thrown into a river. Some were hacked limb from limb with the head being last removed. For sport they were thrown under the feet of elephants.

Many of the martyrs were Vietnamese catechists and lay Christians. Cothonay, in *Lives of Twenty-six Martyrs of Tonkin* (1913), describes the cruel martyrdom of catechists Francis Mau and Dominic My, tailor Thomas De, and farmers Augustine Moi and Stephen Vinh in 1839. Some hagiography in the telling cannot be ruled out, but the martyrdoms were real and often very cruel.

The fervor and courage in captivity of the tailor and farmers under torture is said to have edified

> all those who came in contact with them . . . They had the
> consolation of bringing back to the Faith many Christians
> who had shown weakness from fear of tortures. Moreover,

many pagans manifested the desire to know and embrace the Catholic religion. The prison, instead of serving to bring Christians to apostasy, was the means of procuring the knowledge of the truth and the grace of Baptism for the pagans. (ibid., 211)

After enduring many tortures without recanting, they were sentenced and executed as

evil-doers who follow the religion of Jesus. Having been admonished many times and punished . . . yet they will not trample the cross under foot. They are to be immediately strangled . . . Soon the procession was to be seen wending its way towards the place of execution . . . All wore a white tunic . . . They wore their cangues, and holding their hands crossed upon their breasts, they prayed with great fervor. When they came to a place outside the town of Co-Me, the workmen sawed off their *cangues*, and the martyrs were stretched upon the earth, and attached to stakes in such a manner that their bodies formed a cross. A silk cord was placed around their necks. At a signal from the Mandarin it was violently drawn by the executioners and the Blessed Martyrs expired, invoking the name of Jesus. (ibid., 219–20)

Here are strong echoes of Hebrews 11:35–40 and of persecution during Roman times.

On June 19, 1988, Pope John Paul II canonized 117 Catholics, together named The Vietnam Martyrs. Of these, ninety-six were Vietnamese priests and lay Catholics. The rest were foreign missionary priests. This act greatly irritated Vietnam's Communist rulers.

Catholics: The Colonial Period

Long after the Catholic Church was established, there was some unfortunate collusion between the church and France which established colonial power over Indochina, including Vietnam, in the 1860s. Yet the church, already more than two centuries old, continued to grow and through its schools had a disproportionate positive influence on Vietnamese society.

In the twentieth century, after the Geneva Accords divided Vietnam at the seventeenth parallel in 1954, the Catholic Church became a bastion of anti-communism in the south. South Vietnam's first president, Ngo Dinh Diem, was an ardent Catholic. He strongly favored Catholics in his administration and military. His sister-in-law, Madame Nhu, who served as first lady to the unmarried president, worked to impose Catholic values on South Vietnam. This helped lead to a major Buddhist revolt that culminated in the self-immolation of several monks. After surviving coup attempts in 1960 and 1962, President Diem's own military officers deposed and assassinated him in 1963 with quiet American complicity.

Following these tragic events, one could say that the Catholic Church was freed from the political burden of too close an identification with the state, but there remained an understandable, strong antipathy toward atheistic communism. Hence Catholics are held highly suspect by the regime to this day.

Catholics: Since 1975

Following the Communist victory in 1975, the large Catholic Church in the south suffered the confiscation of all its extensive education, medical, and social work infrastructure. Yet all was not lost. During one Canadian church visit in 1986, our delegation was taken to a "government" orphanage in Thu Duc, not far from Ho Chi Minh City. The peaceful faces and demeanor of the plainclothes women serving the orphans made me suspect they were nuns. Momentarily alone with one woman as our group turned a corner, I pulled my gold cross necklace from my shirt. She smiled widely and made the sign of the cross!

Following their 1975 victory, the Communist authorities resorted to the ruse of creating a "patriotic" Catholic Church. From thousand of priests, government officials selected a few sympathetic to their cause and pretended they spoke for the whole church. Foreign delegations were introduced to these unfaithful priests as representative of Vietnamese Catholics. But the pretense was so thin that almost everyone except the willfully blind could see through it.

The strategy of the Catholic Church has usually been to avoid confrontation and get on quietly with pastoral work. At the same time some highly visible priests, such as Fathers Steven Chan Tin and Thaddeus Nguyen Van Ly, carried on courageous opposition to religious repression in their speaking and their underground publications. It is believed they had the tacit support of the Council of Bishops. The defiant Father Ly has been sentenced to prison several times and as of this writing is on a "health leave" from prison following three strokes.

Since 2007, Catholics have tested the supposed increase in religious freedom by seeking the return of long-confiscated church properties in various parts of the country. In the early months of 2008, thousands of faithful carried candles to and prayed at the former papal embassy and the Thai Ha Redemptorist property in Hanoi. Authorities at first promised negotiations on these property issues, but a final answer appeared on September 19, 2008. As evening fell, bulldozers razed some of the buildings on these properties, and within a couple of days they were turned into public parks! One priest joked that Vietnam should make the *Guinness Book of World Records* for speed in building public parks!

It was the worldwide attention drawn by the Catholic prayer vigils that made the authorities turn the church properties into public parks. But this was only a muted victory, for the top authorities had hoped for great personal profit by the sale of these valuable lands. Spiteful at their loss, they recruited thugs who, with plainclothes police, attacked the remaining chapel on the Redemptorist property, significantly damaging holy objects. The official state media launched brutal attacks and slander on Catholics and their leaders over these property issues. A special target was Hanoi Archbishop Joseph Ngo Van Kiet. The government demanded his removal, angered by the Archbishop's bold statement that it was not in the state's authority to grant or withhold religious freedom. That, the archbishop proclaimed, is a fundamental human right conferred by the Creator God.

In June 2010 Archbishop Kiet (57) mysteriously resigned. He was replaced by Bishop Pierre Nguyen Van Nhon (72), who was approved by the government. Many Catholics were highly suspicious, though the archbishop insisted he resigned of his own volition for "health reasons." Vietnam authorities added to the suspicion when they reported his resignation opened the way for them to move ahead with Vatican relations and accept a nonresident Vatican ambassador based in Singapore.

Additional Catholic property claims attracted many demonstrators in 2009 at the Tam Toa church in Quang Binh province in central Vietnam, and in connection with the demolition of the convent of Sisters of St. Paul Chartres in the southern city of Vinh Long. The sisters there were among the very few willing to care for AIDS patients.

Catholics also regularly complain about the degree of the government's interference in demanding to preapprove seminary students and approve the placement of graduate priests.

In January 2007 high-level talks between Vietnam and the Vatican led to a visit by Vietnamese Prime Minister Nguyen Tan Dung to the Pope in Rome. Then in 2009 Vietnamese President Nguyen Minh Triet visited the Pope. These visits fueled speculation that diplomatic relations might be restored after more than fifty years. Yet, by actions as described above, Vietnam subverts the likelihood.

In spite of all this, the Catholic Church, numbering about eight million, is paying renewed attention to evangelism and is growing. Because of its long history, its large size, and what it stands for, the Catholic Church can be sure the watchful eye of the state will scrutinize its every move for the foreseeable future.

CHAPTER 4

The Coming of the Protestants

A Neglected Corner of the World

Protestants trailed Catholics to Vietnam by three centuries. Of the Protestant Dutch and British whom Alexander de Rhodes met in the Far East in the seventeenth century, he could only comment that "neither one nor the other put themselves to any trouble to convert the pagans, so little love do they have for making Jesus Christ known" (de Rhodes 1966, 193).

It would take the pietist movement, which the reformed state Protestant churches treated with scorn and hostility, and the eighteenth-century Evangelical Awakening to inject into Protestantism a concern for mission.

The nineteenth century, for Protestant mission the "Great Century," had seen Protestant Christianity carried to nearly every major area of the world except French Indochina—now the countries of Vietnam, Laos, and Cambodia.

In 1887 a Canadian, Dr. A. B. Simpson, who was to found the Christian and Missionary Alliance (C&MA), wrote in his magazine *Word, Work and World*, "The southeastern peninsula of Asia has been much neglected. The great kingdom of Annam should be occupied for Christ. Why should it not . . . be one of the first fields for a new aggression by the people of God?" (Reimer 1972, 20).

Finally, in the last decade of the nineteenth century, the first Protestant missionaries set foot on Vietnamese soil.

The Pioneers

They were agents of the British and Foreign Bible Society (BFBS) who first came to Vietnam. Probably the first representative was a French citizen.

In 1890 the name "Bonnet" was attached to the first scripture portion translated into Vietnamese. BFBS agents were known to have distributed scripture portions (mostly in the Chinese language) and used oil lanterns and slides to depict the life of Christ, but they did not start churches.

Eventually, it was through Bonnet of the BFBS that the C&MA was to enter Vietnam in 1911. From its established mission in southern China, the C&MA had started to make forays into Tonkin, now northern Vietnam, in the 1890s. But setbacks and hindrances prevented the C&MA from establishing itself in Vietnam until 1911. That year the obstacles evaporated. In response to an invitation from Bonnet, missionary pioneer R. A. Jaffray led a delegation to Tourane (present-day Danang). Bonnet, who wanted to move to Hanoi, turned over to the C&MA the BFBS property and modest infrastructure. Missionary Paul Hosler took up residence there before the end of 1911.

The approach the C&MA would take was much shaped by R. A. Jaffray. The well-bred son of a Canadian newspaper magnate, he had disappointed his father when he dedicated his life to Christian mission in Asia. He served first in South China, where he became widely known for his publication of a Chinese Bible magazine. Jaffray gave personal oversight to the new work in Vietnam until 1923.

Jaffray's experience in China shaped his strategy in Vietnam. He was concerned that missionaries in the new field of Vietnam should not repeat what he deemed mistakes of missionary financial policy in China. It was a temptation in the colonial period (and still is today) to think that "natives" were too poor to support their own church. This meant churches became dependent on missionary money and limited in their ability to grow. It was much better that they be self-supporting, self-governing, and self-propagating,[8] in the terminology of Henry Venn and Rufus Anderson, prominent missionary thinkers of the day.

A good summary of the approach of early C&MA missionaries came from D. I. Jeffrey (to be distinguished from Jaffray), who arrived in Vietnam in 1918. In some 1963 recollections, he describes the young mission's master plan as follows:

---

8   The fact that the Three-Self Movement was taken under control of the Communist Party in the People's Republic of China in 1951, with tragic consequences for churches, does not invalidate the three-self principle nor diminish its usefulness and urgency as a missionary method.

Institutional work should take its proper place, with primary
emphasis on the planting and growth of indigenous churches. Direct evangelistic preaching of the gospel, translation
of the Bible into the vernacular, the establishment of a Bible
school to train native pastors and evangelists, should all be
started and maintained. The publication of Christian literature should be emphasized.[9]

The work began in 1911 with a single resident missionary. By 1915
the field force had increased to nine when a setback occurred. World War I
hostilities in Europe caused French officials to suspect missionaries with
German-sounding names such as Hosler, Hazenberg, and Morganthaler and
to order missionary work to stop. This reduced the number to five. However,
by 1921 a total of twenty-two missionaries were at work in Vietnam. Jaffray's
policy was to disperse them throughout the long and narrow country with
missionaries taking up residence in Hanoi in the north in 1916 and Saigon
in the south in 1918. The early missionaries had to overcome the suspicion of
French colonial officials and often the outright hostility of Roman Catholic
priests, who considered Protestants heretical. But in 1916 Jaffray, a skillful
diplomat, surprisingly secured the welcome of the French governor-general in
Hanoi to carry on all kinds of missionary work "in the French possessions."

The amazing story of early C&MA missionary work is well told in the
small book *Pen Pictures of Annam and its People* by Grace Hazenburg Cadman
(1920). Clearly reflecting the views of the day, the narrative skillfully outlines
the accomplishments and setbacks of the pioneer missionaries. The book
contains some of the earliest photographs of the mission's work and many fine
line drawings of Vietnam scenes, including everything from "native" peoples
to ornate colonial buildings. Grace Hazenburg, an American, grew up in
South Africa where her parents were missionaries. She first met William
Cadman, her husband-to-be, in Vietnam.

---

9   From some unpublished recollections by missionary D. I. Jeffrey.

From Grace Cadman's Pen Pictures of Annam and its People *(1920).*

William C. Cadman was a Canadian originally from England where he had been a printer by trade. In 1920 he brought a modern printing press to Hanoi where he began producing high quality Christian literature. Literature was a key part of the strategy of the C&MA mission. By 1927 the Evangelical Press under Cadman's supervision was producing five million pages a year.

In 1916 the Cadmans, including Grace who graduated with an MA from a Canadian university and had studied Hebrew and Greek, began translation of the Bible into Vietnamese. With support of the BFBS, they also engaged Vietnamese scholars such as Phan Khoi to help ensure a good literary translation. The first complete Vietnamese Bible came off the press in Hanoi in 1926. Though a number of updated translations have been published recently, the original 1926 version remains the Bible of choice for most Vietnamese Christians to this day.

It was a remarkable missionary achievement to have completed a good translation of the whole Bible within fifteen years of first setting foot on Vietnam's soil. The Cadmans did have the advantage of using the just-completed Roman Catholic parallel Vietnamese-Latin Vulgate Bible. It was published by the Paris Missionary Society in four heavy volumes totaling over three thousand pages between 1913 and 1916—a full three centuries after Catholic missionaries arrived in Vietnam.[10]

The Cadmans were both interned by the Japanese in 1943 and yet remained in Vietnam after the end of World War II. The couple whose missionary legacy in Vietnam looms large both died and were buried in Vietnam—Grace in 1946 and William three years thereafter. Their only child, Agnes, who succumbed to polio at age six, was buried in Hanoi.

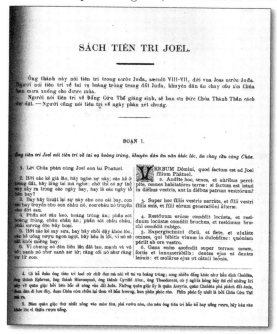

The first page of the book of Joel in the Vietnamese-Latin Vulgate Bible.

A Church Emerges

The first chapel was built in modern-day Danang in 1913; by 1920 it had grown to a congregation of 104! According to a 1917 report the first members included a wide range of people.

---

10 In 1984 I inherited the very set of these Bibles that were used by the Cadmans from missionary D. I. Jeffrey.

> Several young boys from the Sunday school . . . determined
> to follow the Lord in spite of their parents' displeasure, [as
> well as] a daughter and mother, a number of men from the
> student class, two members of the royal family, a railroad
> engineer, and the native preacher who had been a Confu-
> cian scholar. (ibid., 32)

Response was slower in Hanoi, where in 1921, after four years of labor, only seventeen baptized members made up the church there. By the same year a small church had been established in Saigon in the south.

An important part of the foundation, the missionaries agreed, was train- ing Vietnamese pastors. The first training classes were held in Danang in 1919 for four students. In 1921 a more organized school of nine students was opened in a converted horse stable on the Danang station.

The first decade accomplishments were impressive by any standard! By 1921 the twenty-two missionaries scattered in five locations across over one thousand miles of French Indochina had a core of baptized believers in the three main centers of Vietnam. The translation of the Bible was well under way, a school for training pastors had been launched, and a modern printing press had been set up in Hanoi.

In 1922, the year before Jaffray left the scene to open up yet another field for the C&MA in Indonesia, he prophetically told his superiors in New York that God was on the march in Indochina. His prophecy came to pass! The two decades from 1921–1940 saw the baptism of over twenty thousand Vietnamese converts and the emergence of a strong, largely self-supporting, autonomous church. The period climaxed in the first ethnic Vietnamese mis- sionaries being sent to minority tribes in their own country.

The Three Regions

There was, however, a remarkable difference in the speed of growth in the three main regions of what is now the Socialist Republic of Vietnam. They were the northern area (Tonkin), the central area (Annam), and the south- ern area (Cochinchina). One could say, like the parable, that the church grew one hundredfold in the south, sixtyfold in the center, and only thirty- fold in the north.

In part these different rates of growth occurred because the French offered varying degrees of religious freedom in different regions of French Indochina. The 1916 French permission for the C&MA was to work in French "possessions." All of the southern region of Cochinchina was considered a possession, but only the city of Tourane (modern-day Danang) in central Annam, and the cites of Haiphong and Hanoi in the northern Tonkin, were deemed possessions.

Hence missionaries had open access to Cochinchina in the far south, but were restricted in the central and northern colonies. In 1928 strict measures were taken in central Annam to prevent the spread of the gospel. Preachers and colporteurs were fined and imprisoned, Christians' homes were invaded, Bibles confiscated, and stern ultimatums to become Catholic or face punishment were issued.

Posters, as the one quoted below from the missionaries' magazine in 1928 (ibid., 51), were placed on chapel doors, in public markets, and published in Vietnamese newspapers.

Public Notice

According to the decision of the Royal Court, the first month, the fourth day of the third year of King Bao Dai's reign, may it be brought to the remembrance of people that only Roman Catholics may propagate their religion in the Province of Annam.

All other religions are absolutely forbidden, excepting only the different religions that the Annamese people have followed from of old to the present time, which are their ordinary customs and thus not forbidden. Thus all superstitions are prohibited: Christianity, the Gospel, and Cao Daism are all absolutely forbidden.

Whosoever does not obey the above decree shall be punished.

Nhatrang, March 2, 1928

The story of Vietnamese Protestant pastor Phan Dinh Lieu, who was jailed and made to sweep streets, became widely known. When the French Protestant pastor Calas in Hanoi heard of it, he protested this shameful treatment of Protestants to the French governor-general in Hanoi and to the Chamber of Deputies in Paris. An embarrassed French government quickly reversed its policy and leaned on the emperor of Annam to issue a reinterpretation of the Treaty of 1884.

By 1935 most harassment had stopped, even in the strongly Roman Catholics regions of Tonkin. Missionaries considered religious freedom to have arrived. Yet they cited problems associated with it as a main reason for slower growth in central and northern Vietnam.

But in addition to politics, human receptivity was certainly another cause for varying responses. The Vietnamese culture, especially the worship of ancestors, was longest and deepest established in the north. A 1927 missionary report said, "The Tonkinese are holding most tenaciously to their heathen religions, customs, and family ties—only the power of God can break these ties" (ibid., 54).

As Vietnamese migrated southward over the centuries, they became less attached to their traditional beliefs and practices and hence more open to new ideas, including nontraditional religions and the Christian gospel. Further, material life was considerably easier in the south than the north, and churches in the south found it easier to support their own pastors and erect their own churches. Also in the south, people came to faith in whole families, contrary to the Western understanding of one-by-one conversion. This was critically important in a culture where family opposition was a main hindrance to becoming Christian.

Indeed, beliefs and practices associated with ancestor worship were then and are still a great hindrance to Christian conversion. Early missionaries, who correctly analyzed the Cult of the Ancestors as involving the actual worship of ancestral spirits, failed to recognize the positive elements of honoring parents and ancestors which are quite compatible with Christian belief. And so early Protestantism in Vietnam came sometimes to bear the epithet *dao bo ong bo ba*, or "the religion that discards the ancestors." This was an unnecessary hindrance to the gospel.

Nevertheless, the church grew, especially in the south. There spontaneous expansion marked the period from 1925–1932. In 1925 some 940 people were baptized in the city of Mytho, resulting in twelve new churches! The gospel often spread along family lines. People often came from afar and carried the gospel back to their homes. Artisans and tradesmen shared their faith while at work. Laymen gave their time to help evangelists and missionaries start new churches. Converts freely gave land and erected church buildings.

Scores of converts were also attracted to the Christian way because they witnessed the power of Christ in healing diseases. They found in Christianity a release from the depressing and binding fears of their animistic beliefs. The exorcism of demons and spirits was common, practiced by lay Christians as well as evangelists. People were delivered from opium addiction. Sorcerers were converted and became evangelists. It was a New Testament kind of movement in many respects.

The church grew also, albeit more slowly, in central and northern Vietnam. Already in 1929 the churches of the three regions were united in one independent body, the Evangelical Church of Vietnam.

God Sends a Revival

In 1936 four students at the Bible school in Danang began to pray earnestly for revival. Prayer expanded to include most of the student body and persisted for two years. Then, as if to prepare it for the looming war and trials ahead, God visited Vietnam's churches with a major revival in 1938.

The instrument was famed Chinese revivalist John Sung. The American-educated Chinese revivalist aimed his ministry strictly at Christians. At Vinh Long, Saigon, and Danang, the tireless Sung ministered in week-long events, holding forth in three-hour sessions in the morning, afternoon, and evening. He wore out his interpreters and amazed all with his stamina!

At first the reserved and protocol-conscious Vietnamese did not know what to make of Dr. Sung's highly exuberant style. But the Holy Spirit broke through! The result was an outpouring of God's power to purify and renew His people. Leaders and lay people alike experienced deep conviction of sin. Restitutions were made and numerous relationships healed. The powerful preaching of Dr. Sung also burned residual animistic beliefs and practices out of the lives of believers. Missionaries reported they had never seen such spiritual power. For some time thereafter, Vietnamese Christians were greatly renewed in their zeal for evangelism.

For many years, both pastors and lay Christians would recall Dr. Sung's flaming Bible messages and spiritual power as a turning point in their lives.

CHAPTER 5

The Protestant Church during Three Wars

Vietnam was occupied by Imperial Japan in 1941, then forced to fight a long war against colonial France for independence from 1945–1954. Ending with the division of Vietnam at the seventeenth parallel in 1954, that war evolved into a decade-long civil war, greatly exacerbated by massive foreign involvement on both sides. Finally, in 1975 a divided Vietnam was united under communism following the collapse of South Vietnam. One could say Vietnam experienced thirty-five years of war, with few respites! How would the church survive such turmoil and devastation?

The Japanese Occupation (1941–1945)

The Japanese invaded and occupied Vietnam in mid-1941, integrating the country into Japan's "Greater East Asia Cooperative Prosperity Sphere." For the Vietnamese, it was much more like a "devastation sphere."

The Japanese demanded that all missionary activity by foreigners cease. Missionaries in the south were ordered to a central location in Dalat. In 1943 a dozen not freed in a Japanese-American civilian prisoner exchange were interned in the southern city of Mytho. The treatment of the interned missionaries steadily deteriorated. One died in custody. These events prevented missionary support of the Vietnamese churches for a time. Some courageous Vietnamese Christians helped sustain the interned missionaries by bringing them supplies and encouragement.

How did the church survive? Those in the poorer north suffered the most. Eleven of fifty-seven churches were closed for a time. In the south, churches managed to remain open. Without any missionary subsidies available, the better-off churches in the south gave generously in cash and kind to support their hard-pressed Christian coworkers in the north. Prompted by a dream, church president Le Van Thai took up love offerings in a tour of the south, netting four trunks full of valuable goods-in-kind and enabling the northern church to resume ministry.

Christians suffered severely along with their countrymen through the Great Vietnam Famine of 1944–1945. Chief among the causes of the famine was the confiscation of rice by the Japanese and the war-caused destruction of railroads and roads, preventing the shipment of food from the south and center to the north—barely sustainable even in normal times.

Yet without missionary support during World War II, the young Vietnamese church showed itself surprisingly mature. It grew modestly in numbers while also increasing in organizational strength. But now a new crisis awaited. The fires of nationalism began to burn as it appeared independence could become a reality. Would the struggle for independence begun in 1945 have more dire consequences for the church than the Japanese occupation?

The War of Independence (1945–1954)

Ho Chi Minh,[11] leader of the independence movement, rushed to fill the vacuum created by the defeat of Japan and the weakness of France after World War II. He declared the Democratic Republic of Vietnam on September 2, 1945. But sadly, Allied bungling allowed the French to try to recapture their former colonial glory in East Asia. Promises of freedom within a French union proved empty when a French bombardment of Haiphong killed six thousand civilians. The fight for independence was on.

Eight years of savage war ensued. It shattered Vietnam's economy. A seesaw battle between the French and the Viet Minh (which the independence forces called themselves) finally ended when the demoralized French were defeated in the Battle of Dien Bien Phu in 1954. At Geneva, where both the emperor Bao Dai and Ho Chi Minh claimed to speak for all Vietnamese,

---

11 An excellent biography on the life of one of the twentieth century's most remarkable and enigmatic leaders, *Ho Chi Minh* was published by American scholar William J. Duiker (2000). Ho Chi Minh died in 1969. Contrary to his written will which stipulated cremation, Communist leaders decided to put his body on display in a specially built mausoleum in Hanoi's Ba Dinh Square, à la Vladimir Lenin in Moscow and Mao Tse Tung in Beijing.

the great powers decided to divide Vietnam at the seventeenth parallel, making provision for what they hoped would be eventual peaceful reunification.

The Evangelical Church of Vietnam (ECVN) suffered a great setback during this war. In spite of an average of some seven hundred new baptisms per year, the ECVN suffered a net loss of nearly eight thousand baptized believers from 1942–1952. People disappeared because of the massive disruption of war, causing believers to be scattered, but also because of reversions, some due to the attraction of the nationalist cause. Many church buildings were destroyed, especially in the north. In the south, anarchy and lawlessness ensued as Cao Dai and Hoa Hao militias joined the fray for their own reasons.

The ECVN took a position of official neutrality during the War of Independence. In 1946, not long after the declaration of the Democratic Republic of Vietnam, ECVN's leader, the Reverend Le Van Thai, had an audience with Ho Chi Minh. The revolutionary leader, whose Communist leanings were still veiled at that time, tried to elicit the official support of the ECVN for his government. Rev. Thai insisted that the church would remain officially neutral in matters political, but nuanced his answer by saying that many individual Christians were doing their part for the independence struggle.

Though they wanted neither French domination nor communism, Vietnamese Protestants were apparently more ready to risk the latter than endure the former. But the reluctance to take sides meant that individual Christians were mistreated and sometimes imprisoned by both sides. Nationalist forces often pressured Christians behind Viet Minh lines to join the fight against the foreign occupiers. And some did so willingly.

For others in contested areas, who lived under one government at night and another during the day, Romans 13:1 enjoining Christians to obey "the governing authorities" provided insufficient guidance. Further complicating the feelings of Vietnamese Christians was the knowledge that it was American munitions and aid that enabled the French to continue their military campaign.

Halfway through this war, it became clear the independence forces had taken a sharp turn in the Communist direction. In 1951 Ho Chi Minh began to purge the resistance movement of non-Communists. Even Protestants who were involved in the resistance or who were sympathetic were sidelined. Pressure mounted on those behind Viet Minh lines to abandon their faith.

When C&MA missionaries resumed their activity after the defeat of the Japanese, their movements were confined to the French-controlled zones, though they also responded to needs behind Viet Minh lines. Their main work during the new war became the recovery of scattered congregations and their rehabilitation. In 1947 discouraged church leaders requested the mission to resume financial subsidies. Missionaries reluctantly complied, reversing their self-support policy but hoping it would be a temporary measure. But they were obliged to continue because of the ongoing devastation of the long war. Painful steps, which almost ruptured church and missionary relationships, were taken toward the end of the war as support was gradually decreased in order to encourage self-support.

The Geneva Accords of 1954 divided Vietnam in two, putting the North behind a Communist curtain for years to come. For a short time people were allowed to follow their political persuasion and move to the North or South as they desired. The hundreds of thousands, mainly Catholics and Protestants, who went south dwarfed the handful that went north.

The division of the country also divided the Evangelical Church of Vietnam. From this time forward it would be necessary to speak of the ECVN(N) and the ECVN(S).

The War of Independence left the ECVN(S) battered and bruised, both numerically and spiritually. There was virtually no net growth during the period. The C&MA mission to the Vietnamese had been reduced to twenty-two missionaries, the same number as in 1921. Things began to look a bit better toward the end of the war, and even better days with peace coming were anticipated by all. Unfortunately, a new war by the North against the South was already in the making.

The Decade after the War of Independence

South Vietnam enjoyed five years of relative peace and stability after the division of the country in 1954. This was followed, however, by increasing instability during the next five.

Vietnamese churches and their supporting missionaries took advantage of the quiet to evangelize and start new churches in provinces that previously had few or none—with some success. They aimed at Quang Tri and Thua Thien provinces just below the seventeenth-parallel dividing line. The area was quite ironically called a "demilitarized zone."

More success was had in Quang Ngai province on the central coast. Vigorous evangelism in coastal fishing villages among strongly animistic Vietnamese led to a number of converts and new churches. This advance turned into a small people movement to Christian faith as a result of two miracles. One was the testimony of a Mrs. Huu, who was blind but miraculously had her sight restored.[12] In the other case, a shaman who was converted to Christian faith became an ardent witness to the power of the Christian God.

The opportunity to do unrestricted evangelism in the rural areas, not possible during the War of Independence, led also to many new churches being planted in other parts of the country. But the peace was not to last.

South Vietnam's Catholic President, Ngo Dinh Diem, struggled against massive odds, at first with some success, in bringing stability to his nation. But from 1960 onward, political stability decreased, culminating with the assassination of Diem in 1963. Then as coup followed coup, Communists began to reach for control of South Vietnam. Southern Communists, called Viet Cong, aided by the North and its allies, employed politics and terrorism, rendering insecure vast rural areas of the South.

The Vietnam War/The American War

American involvement in Vietnam began with well-intentioned efforts to prop up the government in the South. Involvement began under President Eisenhower, though he warned against military intervention. President Kennedy sent a few thousand "advisors" and modest aid. President Johnson used a controversial incident in the Gulf of Tonkin in 1964 to obtain congressional authority to aid a nation threatened by communism. At the peak, the Americans had half a million military personnel on the ground, at sea, and in the air of Vietnam. In 1969 President Nixon changed US policy and tried to "Vietnamize" the war—by which he meant reducing American troops and enabling the South Vietnamese to fight on their own.

At the Paris Peace Accords in 1973, the North Vietnamese agreed to cease aggression, and the Americans agreed to withdraw entirely. The Americans pulled out. But the North Vietnamese had no intention of keeping

---

12 I visited a very ill Mrs. Huu in the summer of 1971 in a seaside village in Quang Ngai, just days before she died. When I asked about her sight, she affirmed, "Yes, the Lord gave me light for my eyes."

their promise. They ramped up their efforts to take over the South, finally succeeding on April 30, 1975, when South Vietnam collapsed after a massive invasion. Vietnam was reunited under communism in a country now named the Socialist Republic of Vietnam.

The Horrors of War

For a witness to a war, it is cold and clinical to just list the main political markers and outcomes. It is not possible to imagine the actual horrors of warfare without seeing and experiencing them.

There is no situation that humans create that is beyond God's redemption. However, war is the worst way mankind has devised to settle differences. Even in so-called wars of necessity, the good guys also do very bad things; barbarism boils up and rarely if ever do armies live up to the standards of the Geneva Convention, let alone the Christian "just war" theory. This was true in Vietnam.

Incredible amounts of human creativity, time, talent, and money go into destruction and into devising efficient machines and methods of finding and killing the enemy. Normally, the side that inflicts the most damage on the other wins! Yet, in the case of Vietnam, the ultimate in modern technology and never-ending resources did not prevail.

The toll of human deaths, wounded and crippled bodies, forever-scarred spirits and souls, women deprived of husbands, children of fathers, and collateral social ills make war an evil that not only inflicts immeasurable immediate cost and pain, but keeps on wreaking personal and societal havoc for years to come. All social institutions, including the church, in the midst of war are heavily burdened and much depleted.

How Did the Christian Cause Fare during the Wars?

Let's start by inquiring about missionary efforts. Remarkably these grew significantly during this war, even in number of personnel, at least until the Tet Offensive in 1968.

The only mission other than the C&MA to enter Vietnam before World War II was the Seventh Day Adventists (SDA). Arriving in 1929, they directed much of their proselytizing at ECVN followers. After forty years of work, in 1970 they reported just over two thousand members in ten churches.

More mainstream evangelical efforts followed after World War II. One was led by Gordon and Laura Smith. This dynamic couple first came to Vietnam as pioneer C&MA missionaries to Vietnam's ethnic minorities in the Central Highlands. The Smiths were ahead of their time in the use of modern mission promotion techniques such as movies. One movie called "Light in the Jungle" vividly illustrated their work to supporters back home. Both Smiths published popular books such as *The Blood Hunters: A Narrative of Pioneer Missionary Work Among the Tribes of French Indo-China* (G. Smith 1942) *and Gongs in the Night* (L. Smith 1943). The books vividly described primitive customs such as sawing off the teeth of prepubescent girls for beauty. Gordon, a serious missionary anthropologist, also published books such as *The Missionary and Primitive Man* (G. Smith 1947). His wide knowledge of Vietnam's Montagnards led a number of secular anthropologists to seek him out.

The Smiths, after parting ways with the C&MA, came back to Vietnam under the auspices of the World Evangelization Crusade (WEC) in 1956. In 1971 most WEC missionaries transferred to the United World Mission (UWM). A church organization called the Vietnam Christian Mission grew out of this work, today counting about 250 congregations and working among twenty tribal groups. In 2007 it became the first church after the ECVN organizations to receive legal recognition by the government.

The entrance into Vietnam of the Mennonite Central Committee for medical and social work in 1954 paved the way for the coming of the Eastern Mennonite Board of Missions and Charities years later in 1957. Southern Baptists from America arrived in 1959.[13] A decade later they had two thousand baptized believers in twenty-three congregations. The Assemblies of God arrived in 1972.

Besides these modest additions to evangelistic missionary work came another strong expression of evangelical concern: to respond to the massive social needs generated by war. World Vision and World Relief, for example, developed huge programs of assistance for wounded soldiers, the many internally displaced people uprooted in battles, and Communist military prisoners. Along with other Christian organizations, they sponsored numerous schools and medical clinics, did development work, and engaged

---

13 The history of Southern Baptists in Vietnam combined with the personal experiences of missionary Sam James is told in his book *Servants on the Edge of History* (2005).

in disaster relief. They often engaged experienced Vietnam missionaries in this work and, as much as feasible, local churches. Together these significant and sustained efforts should correct the false notion of some that evangelicals were only interested in souls and not in human need.

The C&MA, for its part, greatly increased its number of missionaries in Vietnam in the late 1950s and 1960s. In 1971 there were forty-two missionaries working with ethnic Vietnamese and a comparable number with the Montagnards in the Central Highlands. To meet the challenge posed by Vietnam's many tribal groups, the C&MA had organized a separate Montagnard mission in 1953, but political considerations led to joining the ethnic Vietnamese and Montagnard missions back together again in 1959.

The Montagnards

Vietnam's indigenous tribes in the Central or Western Highlands are collectively called Montagnards (French for "mountain people").[14] They belong to two ethno-linguistic families—Mon–Khmer and Malayo–Polynesian—the latter, interestingly, coming centuries ago from islands in the Pacific.

The first missionaries to the Montagnards found them receptive to the gospel. Long bound by oppressive beliefs in malevolent spirits and impoverished by the expensive rituals needed to placate them, many of the animistic Montagnards readily embraced the liberating gospel. Their lives and cultures were radically transformed. Among the most evangelized tribes are the Koho, Ede, Jarai, Bahnar, Stieng, and Mnong. C&MA missionaries, with much help from Wycliffe Bible Translators, translated the Scriptures into these and other languages.

The story of the birth and growth of the Koho tribal church is told in a popular missionary classic called *The Bamboo Cross* (Dowdy 1964). In it, Koho Christians tell stories of protection from Communist attacks by angelic forces and about other miracles and martyrs. By the time the Vietnam War ended, these minority people made up a full third of the ECVN(S), though they constituted only about 13 percent of the population.

---

14 Two scholarly volumes by American anthropologist Gerald C. Hickey (1982a and 1982b) provide a full social and political history of the ethnic minorities of Vietnam's Western Highlands up to 1976. In the 1970s Hickey and I enjoyed long discussions on the Montagnards over lunches in Bangkok.

Montagnards, including many Christians, were recruited into the fight against communism during the Vietnam War. Americans considered the Montagnards their best soldiers and most trustworthy allies. Unfortunately, this association was to greatly complicate life for the Montagnards in the long term.

Montagnards long suffered strong discrimination and injustice at the hands of the dominant Vietnamese, regardless of which government was in power. Montagnard independence aspirations were not a surprising result. A liberation movement called FULRO, a French acronym meaning "front for the liberation of oppressed peoples," was born. It was active from the 1960s and eventually ceased to exist in 1992, long after the formal end of the war, when a bedraggled remnant in the jungles of Cambodia gave up their arms to a UN representative. Interestingly, their Christian faith was very much intact!

Many of the FULRO leaders were Christians. This is not surprising, as they were among the few educated Montagnards and had come to an understanding of human dignity and value from the Christian gospel. The FULRO movement was betrayed in negotiations with the former Vietnam regime and eventually brutally crushed by the Communists. But, until the present time, Montagnard aspirations for justice and their potential resistance to oppression remains a cause for intense Communist suspicion against all Montagnard Christians.

In 2001 and 2004, extensive Montagnard demonstrations in the Western Highlands against confiscation of their traditional lands and lack of religious freedom shocked the Vietnam government. These "uprisings," attributed to instigation by some US-based, one-time FULRO activists, were brutally crushed by massive military force.[15] The 2001 events are described in a Human Rights Watch publication, *Repression of Montagnards: Conflicts over Land and Religion in Vietnam's Central Highlands* (2002).

---

15 In the early 1990s, an exiled former FULRO leader in South Carolina, Kok K'sor, began to popularize the use of the term "Degar" to refer collectively to Vietnam's ethnic minorities in the Central Highlands. Degar is actually an Ede language term derived from *anak ede gar* and is variously said to mean "people of all tribes" or "children of the mountains." Since the Vietnamese language does not have a final "r," the ethnic Vietnamese shortened it to *Dega*. The Vietnam government politicized "Dega" in the term *Tin Lanh Dega* ("Dega Protestantism") which includes for them any and all ethnic minority Christians they suspect of advocating for minority rights and seeking redress for injustices. Such activity is considered subversive and dangerous.

Innovative Wartime Mission and Evangelism

In addition to the usual methods of evangelism such as evangelistic meetings, gospel broadcasting, and literature distribution, missionaries developed a special outreach to Vietnam's large military forces. The pioneer was missionary Ruth Jeffrey. The wife of earlier mentioned D. I. Jeffrey, she was also the daughter of famous China missionary Jonathan Goforth. A tireless worker, she secured permission to visit and witness in military hospitals and distribute Christian literature near the end of the War of Independence.

In the early 1960s, two dynamic C&MA missionaries, Garth Hunt and Jim Livingston, launched an extensive ministry to Vietnam's huge military establishment. With support from World Vision and others, they became the largest distributor of crutches and wheelchairs to South Vietnam's war-wounded. They often accompanied these distributions with evangelistic preaching and the distribution of New Testaments and scripture portions especially printed for the military by the Pocket Testament League. Those who indicated they wanted to become Christians were taught basic doctrine. Hunt, Livingston, and other missionaries also distributed New Testaments to thousands of military recruits. In these ways, tens of thousands of young men heard the gospel and were given New Testaments, influencing an entire generation. Missionaries were also instrumental in initiating a chaplaincy service in the Vietnamese military.

The Vietnam War, time and again, uprooted people in battle zones and forced them into wretched refugee camps. Although intended to be temporary, these camps often lasted a long time. Both missionaries and Vietnamese Christians often brought material aid and spiritual encouragement to these beleaguered refugees. In the mid-1960s they planted a significant number of new churches among these uprooted people.

The evangelistic vision of both the ECVN(S) and its supporting missionaries came to be expressed in the late 1960s in a program called "Evangelism Deep and Wide" (EDW). It was partly sparked by missionaries who had searched around the world for effective evangelism methods and models. They borrowed from a model in Latin America called "Evangelism in Depth," revising and tailoring it to Vietnam. The vision came to be adopted by top ECVN(S) leaders, especially President Doan Van Mieng. He became an enthusiastic proponent of EDW when the Lord gave him a vision for ten million souls! EDW enjoyed some success, but organizational shortcomings and the surrounding war prevented its wide implementation.

Another evangelistic method was the use of mobile vans equipped with movie projectors and sound systems supplied by the Pocket Testament League. With effective Vietnamese evangelists, these vans circulated to markets and parks, attracting huge crowds, showing Moody Science and other films, preaching the gospel, and distributing literature.

In spite of the war, many local church "witnessing bands" continued their faithful work. Long a favored method of evangelism, the bands went out on Sundays, witnessing to individuals and contributing to slow but steady growth of churches in Vietnam.

The High Cost of Serving Christ

I was to witness firsthand the high cost of serving Christ in a war. During the 1968 Tet Offensive, after an attack which came within meters of our house, I took my wife and children to safety in Nhatrang. I then quickly returned to our post in the coastal town of Phan Thiet. Unable to go into town because of continued fighting and air strikes there, I paced around the small airport with a transistor radio held to my ear.

That is how I heard the stunning news that a number of missionaries had been killed in Banmethuot in the Central Highlands. They could only be my colleagues! I hitchhiked back to Nhatrang on the first military flight to join a large contingent of missionaries who had gathered there for safety. From there, two colleagues and I flew up to Banmethuot as soon as we could.

The Banmethuot missionary compound, established in the 1950s, held four substantial homes, a large church, and a leprosarium that had been moved there from the countryside in 1962. That year the Viet Cong abducted three missionaries, forcing the move to the more secure town. Missionaries Archie Mitchell, Dr. Ardell Vietti, and Dan Gerber were never seen again.

The compound at which we arrived was devastated. The two-story houses had been blown up, sometimes only a corner or some walls remaining. The smoke and smell of destruction and death engulfed us. Traumatized Ede Christians quietly joined us to tell what had happened.

The invading Communist soldiers had come at night. They placed satchel charges by the house of missionary Carolyn Griswold and detonated them. Carolyn's father, Leon, recently retired, had joined her to volunteer his services. He was instantly killed, but Carolyn remained barely alive, trapped under a cement beam. The remaining missionaries abandoned their houses and took refuge in a bunker they made by cleaning out a garbage pit in the back of the property. The other houses were blown up next, showering debris on the bunker.

One of the missionaries in the bunker, Bob Ziemer, emerged holding a white towel, intending to negotiate with the Communist soldiers. Before he could speak he was felled with a bullet in the head. His body slumped across a low clothesline. What happened next is not completely clear, but it appears that soldiers approached the bunker, throwing in hand grenades and firing AK–47s. Remaining in the bunker were Bob's wife Marie, Ruth Wilting, a single missionary nurse, and Ed and Ruth Thompson, a missionary couple.

Miraculously, Marie Ziemer survived that attack. Staggering badly wounded from the bunker, she was left to wander about, looking for help. The three missionaries in the bunker were instantly killed.

A counterattack followed shortly after. US soldiers helped free Carolyn Griswold, trapped under the beam, and evacuated her along with Marie Ziemer by helicopter to a military hospital in coastal Nhatrang. Carolyn died of her wounds on arrival, but Marie Ziemer survived and lives to this day. The US military also picked up the body of Bob Ziemer and repatriated it to his native Ohio.

The author, fourth from the left, stands beside missionary colleagues Gene Evans and Dick Phillips.

As we heard the heartbreaking details of the story, standing near the fateful bunker, we asked ourselves what we should do about the three bodies that lay therein. It did not seem right to us that the bodies of those who had given their lives in the service of Christ should repose in a garbage pit! A US Army mortician we consulted informed us that we should be able to move the bodies even though they been dead for about ten days. So we decided to disinter the bodies for reburial near the large landmark Ede church, damaged but still intact. We hired men to dig graves and bought red wooden coffins.

We then set about to uncover our colleagues' bodies. Removing about a foot of earth, we came upon some dark plastic covering the bodies. A soldier had covered them with a body bag. As we peeled back the bag we found the body of Ed Thompson in a kneeling position over his wife. There was a row of bullet holes down the middle of his back.

To the surprise of the mortician advising us, we were unable to move the bodies. He said they had reached the charred stage in which they would break apart if moved. Our colleagues would lie where they had fallen. We tidied up the rubbish and debris that lay everywhere and salvaged bricks from the blown-up house to delineate the gravesite. A clothesline pole served as a perfect cross.

We stood shoulder to shoulder—three missionaries, a handful of Vietnamese Christians, Montagnard Christians, and US soldiers. Together in a simple and tearful service we memorialized our colleagues who had given their lives serving Christ. For me all vestiges of romance in serving in a dangerous war zone disappeared. It could cost the ultimate price. It had cost the ultimate price!

The Thompson children with Vietnamese and tribal church leaders at their parents' burial site. Dr. David Thompson with wife Becki and daughter Rachael stand to the left of the flowers. To the right are Laurel, Judy, Tom and Dale.

A memorial was later built to mark this burial site. It remains, though now in dilapidated condition, in what is now a compound of government medical buildings. The high cultural Vietnamese respect for ancestors and tombs meant it was not demolished. In December 2009, forty-two years after their parents' death, Vietnamese authorities finally permitted the Thompsons' five children to visit the site for the first time.

Also captured in Banmethuot during the Tet Offensive in 1968, and marched away never to be seen again, were C&MA missionary nurse Betty Olsen and Wycliffe missionary Hank Blood. Communist guerillas tore Hank from his wounded wife, Vange, and his children. Captured at the same time was a US official, Mike Benge. He alone survived the long and brutal jungle trek to the north and was freed with other US prisoners in 1973. He provided information for the story of Betty Olsen's excruciating death, told in James and Marti Hefley's book *No Time for Tombstones: Life and Death in the Vietnamese Jungle* (1974). Service in Vietnam cost the lives of others too. Their stories are told in fascinating detail by James Hefley in *By Life or by Death* (1969).

The deaths and sacrifices of missionaries at Banmethuot stirred the evangelical community worldwide as had the missionary deaths in Congo in 1964 and the Auca missionary massacre in South America in 1956.

In March 1975, just weeks before the Communist victory, misfortune again struck missionaries in Banmethuot. Communist soldiers captured seven missionaries and one of their children, then marched and transported them to a northern prison camp. They included, notably, Betty Mitchell, wife of Archie Mitchell, who had been captured in the same area thirteen years earlier. Also taken were C&MA missionaries Norm and Joan Johnson and Dick and Lil Phillips, and Wycliffe missionaries John and Carolyn Miller with their youngest daughter LuAnne. After 234 days of captivity they were finally freed from their North Vietnam prison and reunited with their children. Their remarkable story of survival is told by James and Marti Hefley in a book entitled *Prisoners of Hope* (1976). A gripping first-person account of this captivity is told by Carolyn Miller in *Captured!* (1977).

The missionary deaths and captivities in 1968 caused soul searching back home. C&MA leaders in the US received considerable advice from their supporting churches about their missionaries in a war zone. Some said to bring them home. For a time, all women missionaries and children were ordered to evacuate to nearby Thailand. Yet, in spite of the now freshly demonstrated, deadly dangers of war, many missionaries counted the cost and resumed their work. However, after the deaths and abductions in Banmethuot in 1968, about half of the C&MA missionaries did not return to serve after they went on home-leave. Other newer missions also saw a decline in their Vietnam staff.

The Vietnam War was a guerilla war with no clear lines or fronts. Large parts of the country were controlled by the Viet Cong, especially by night, and were not even considered safe for foreigners during the day.

Yet most missionaries were more than fully occupied in the cities and towns, in refugee camps, and in ministry to the military. Some ministered in medical clinics and hospitals. Some worked diligently in producing Christian literature and gospel radio broadcasts. Some taught English as an evangelistic entrée. Missionary professors of the C&MA also taught in the large Bible school on the ocean in Nhatrang, which their organization had helped the ECVN(S) to build in the early 1960s.

Vietnam Churches in Wartime

The neutral position proclaimed by the ECVN(S) during the War of Independence proved hard to maintain in the life-and-death struggle between the Southern Republic and the Communist North. A universal military draft in the South meant that many young Christian men were obliged to join their countrymen in the fighting. Christians took their share of casualties. As a young missionary I remember being deeply touched at Protestant funerals for young soldiers killed in combat and the outpouring of uncontrolled grief from their widows and fatherless children.

While people make adjustments to living with a war, nothing is really ever normal. All struggled to make a meager living. The hardship extended to churches, many of which had a difficult time supporting their pastors, let alone initiating outreach ministries. But people pressed on. In Saigon, for example, the ECVN(S), with support from the C&MA mission, opened twelve new churches between March 1972 and March 1975.

It is worth noting that Vietnamese churches and Christian institutions such as orphanages often benefited from the concern and largesse of the US military. Chaplains brought not only food and other material help but involved their men, volunteering their service to aid needy people.

What about evangelism and starting new churches during the prelude to and during the Vietnam War? It can be said with certainty that political confusion, terrorist insurgency, and bitter civil war did not stop the expansion of the church. From 1963–1970 the number of baptized members in the ECVN(S) more than doubled. So did the number of churches!

The 1971 Revival

God visited the ECVN(S), especially the Montagnard churches, with a revival in 1971. As had the 1938 revival, this one too, in retrospect, seemed given by God to prepare His people for heavy hardship not far ahead.

Though revivals are by nature unexplainable visits of God's power among His people, it is instructive to try to trace their origins. A firsthand account of this revival, here summarized, is told in participant missionary Orrel Steinkamp's small volume, *The Holy Spirit in Vietnam* (1973).

In 1971 a number of C&MA missionaries sensed a strong need for renewal and a hunger for more spiritual power. They prayed diligently for such. They experienced a special visitation of the Holy Spirit during their May 1971 annual conference, under the ministry of a visiting American pastor, the Reverend William Allen of Mansfield, Ohio.

Steinkamp returned to his teaching post at the ECVN(S)'s Nhatrang Bible School. In his own quest for more spiritual authenticity he met at a nearby base with American soldiers who were part of the Jesus People movement then flourishing in California. To his own surprise he felt led of God to add prayer for healing of the sick and the exorcising of demons to his ministry, which he did.

Back at the Bible school, Steinkamp had felt led to ask the dean if he could create a course on the history of revivals. The idea, although not enthusiastically received, was not declined, and so Steinkamp went ahead.

Steinkamp describes his History of Revivals class in Room 5 on December 3, 1971, as beginning in a normal way. However, the teacher of another class had cancelled class that day, and his students came to Room 5 to hear a student report on the Indonesia revival of the 1960s. This meant that half of the school's

117 students were in the class. They heard a detailed account of the 1960s revival in Indonesia, replete with stories of healings and many other miracles.

When he had completed his report, the presenter asked his fellow students to pray for revival in Vietnam, and for it to begin at the Bible school. After about ten minutes of normal, quiet prayer, one student began to pray and weep and confess specific sins. Then the room erupted in spontaneous and simultaneous prayer. The word spread quickly, and soon almost all the other students joined those in Room 5. They were visited by a "strong wind of the Spirit," says Steinkamp. Both the foreign missionaries and Vietnamese teachers were soon engulfed in this revival as well. Powerful manifestations continued late into the night and the days following. It also quickly spread to the young people in a nearby church.

The revival particularly affected some Montagnard students at the Bible school, and it spread through them to the Central Highlands. A Vietnamese missionary to the Koho tribe, Pastor Truong Van Tot, also played a key role. He was just back from studies in the US. There he also had heard much about the Indonesia revival, and it led him to make things right in his own life and to reconcile with others. So when the five Koho students who had experienced the revival came home for the Christmas break, he encouraged them to spread their spiritual fervor far and wide. Indeed, a Vietnamese evangelist who witnessed the events said, "The highlands are aflame!"

Revival spread to other tribes in the highlands too. Missionaries accepted at face value the account of the raising from the dead of an Ede lad named Y Djhang through the prayer of Pastor Y Tang. Y Tang had been a language teacher to a Wycliffe missionary and was later called to be a pastor.

Steinkamp summarized the revival as follows:

> Doubt has turned into expectancy, pride has been humbled, sin has been confessed. Wherever there is criticism, doubt and holding back, the revival has been quenched or not come at all. Its chief characteristics have been prayer, public confession of sin, the filling of the Holy Spirit, boundless joy, daring faith, various miracles, and bold witness. The maturity of the revival is shown in that miracles have not been sought. They have occurred only as people got right with God and the Lord chose to send such miracles. Healings however have been sought and secured through faith. (ibid., 77)

A Significant Christian Census

In 1973, less than two years before the Communist victory, the Lausanne
Committee for World Evangelization commissioned me to prepare a profile
on Vietnamese Protestantism in preparation for the first Lausanne Congress
in Switzerland. As it was still possible to travel and connect widely, I was able
to compile what would be the last pre-Communist era complete census for
Vietnam's Protestant community. It became a benchmark by which to measure subsequent church growth.[16]

The census found that the ECVN(S) had a Christian community figure
of 127,505 and that another twenty-six thousand believers were scattered
among eight small denominations. If one adds the generous estimate of six
thousand Protestants remaining in then-inaccessible North Vietnam, both
Vietnams had a Protestant population of approximately 160,000.

---

16   The author produced *South Vietnam: Status of Christianity Country Profile* for the inaugural Lausanne Congress on World Evangelization in 1974.

CHAPTER 6

The "Fall of Saigon" or "Liberation Day"?

On April 30, 1975, the symbolism of the North Vietnamese tank crashing through the gate of the old palace in Saigon and a formal surrender by the remnants of the old regime clearly marked a new era for all of Vietnam.

All missionaries either left or were evacuated except a few of a pacifist persuasion who chose to stay. A year later they also were "invited to leave." The events around the "fall" or "liberation," depending on which side you were on, fostered confusion and deep fear for many Vietnamese Christians.

The confusion in the church at the time remains an embarrassment; very little serious reflection about that situation has occurred. However, in 1995, twenty years after the fall of Saigon, one Vietnamese pastor collected the documents of the ECVN(S) during those tumultuous times. The documents, compiled under the translated title *Twenty Years After* by Pastor Tran Thai Son,[17] show clearly there was no overall strategy or plan on how to react to a Communist victory. Hence confusion reigned.

The ECVN(S) president, Rev. Doan Van Mieng, had been strongly encouraged by a Korean pastor friend, citing the Korean experience, to leave Vietnam in the event of a Communist takeover. In the end, Pastor Mieng decided to stay, though most of his large family left.

In the panic, the son of one nationally prominent pastor, a South Vietnam Air Force pilot, "commandeered" a C-130 transport plane. He landed it on a highway to rescue his parents and family, along with another pastor, a prominent lay Christian man, and their families. They even loaded a car before escaping to Singapore! There were also rumors that some foreign

---

17 This document, privately published and circulated by the author, caused controversy because it recalled some church actions which proved regrettable in hindsight.

organizations had money and contingency plans to rescue their staff and certain church leaders. These rumors gave rise to anxiety and gave false hope.

A week before the fall, the ECVN(S) superintendent of the Saigon area, Nguyen Van Quan, published a bulletin in the newspapers saying there was no plan for ECVN(S) leaders to leave. The statement added that if any pastors left, it was their individual choice, not the policy of the ECVN(S). National leaders made no such statement.

Hundreds of Vietnamese Christians, including some pastors, scrambled to join the exodus. Some were successful. Missionaries were torn concerning their duty to Vietnamese Christians. Two missionaries, fearing an imminent bloodbath for Christians, returned during the confused final days to rescue pastors and other Christians. Larry Ward, founder of Food for the Hungry, and C&MA missionary Garth Hunt miraculously managed to get more than 1,700 people's names recorded on the passenger lists of US Air Force C-130 transport planes bound for the Philippines (Rohrer 1984, 159–70).

After all other missionaries had left, Tom Stebbins returned to Vietnam at the last moment from home leave in the US. On April 28, just two days before the fall, he flew to Saigon via a US Air Force C-130 from the Philippines with orders from C&MA officials to try to secure the evacuation of some selected Christian leaders and their families, ninety-one people in all. But he found some two hundred Christians, and pastors with families, assembled at the International Church on Tran Cao Van Street near the US Embassy, and was given a list of an additional three hundred waiting in their homes. According to Stebbins' own account (Cowles 1976, 108–12), he assured the anxious, waiting Vietnamese Christians: "I told my wife . . . I was willing to sacrifice even my life if I could save even one of you. Your lives are worth no less than mine." He worked feverishly to prepare manifests for their evacuation by the US military, but at midnight the embassy doctor warned him that the evacuation was about to end. He phoned the waiting leaders to tell them that time had run out and that he was leaving. Stebbins then boarded one of the last helicopters to leave the rooftop of the US Embassy, just thirty-four hours after his arrival. He later reflected, "No one will ever know the sorrow that has torn my heart or the flood of tears I have shed for . . . those of our brethren who were left behind. I would gladly have stayed if my staying had meant their evacuation (ibid., 111)."

Some missionaries felt it was a serious theological misunderstanding, if not betrayal, to try to take the pastor-shepherds away from the sheep in a time of trouble. Only a tenth or so of the ECVN(S)'s five hundred pastors and leaders left at that time. Those pastors who tried to leave but failed found their vulnerability had been considerably increased. Warily accepted back by their flocks, they were obliged to attempt to explain their reasons for wanting to leave.

In order to try to avoid the possible negative consequences of their pastors' flight from Vietnam, the executive committee of the ECVN(S) decided to excommunicate them. In a special meeting just a week after the fall, the committee passed such a resolution, naming and excommunicating twenty-five pastors and evangelists who had left—or had attempted to do so. In one sad episode shortly after the fall, a pastor tried to sell thousands of New Testaments as scrap paper! Fear and desperation filled many.

After April 30, 1975, one can say Vietnam fell behind a thick "bamboo curtain" and was to remain there by the decision of Vietnam's Communist leaders until the curtain was cracked a decade later.

The "Dark Decade"

The "Dark Decade"[18] is a name given by Vietnamese to the first ten years following the Communist takeover of the South. It was not long before the North Vietnamese removed the fiction that what had happened in the South was a successful civil uprising of the indigenous southern Communists called the Viet Cong. Northerners quickly pushed the Viet Cong aside and took over the South, earning the deep resentment of southerners, even southern Communists. Northern soldiers, long indoctrinated about the hardships of American oppression, had been completely surprised by the material well-being they found in the south. They fell quickly to looting what to them were unbelievable riches.

The imposition of Communist collectivism of rice farming proved much worse than mere looting, however. The once-prosperous south quickly experienced food shortages that soon brought Vietnam to the brink of outright

---

18 Very little about church affairs during the pressured first decade after the Communist takeover has been published. My sources include some personal written accounts of people who still wish to remain anonymous and many private interviews.

famine. Until 1979 many were chronically hungry, often forced to feed on the most inadequate and the poorest of foods.

The adroit Communist leaders, shocked at the awful results of their policy, reversed themselves and allowed farmers ninety-nine-year tenancy of land—effectively ownership—and the ability to pass land on to their children. Within three years of that policy change, Vietnam became the world's third largest exporter of rice!

The collapse of the economy was even more devastating for urban dwellers. In towns and cities, a third to half of small businesses shut their doors. Hungry and poorly clothed men, women, and children slept on streets near boarded-up buildings, hoping for some shelter.

Hundreds of thousands who had served in the military forces of the former regime, as well as one-time employees of the government of that regime—both categories including many Christians—received mass sentences to "reeducation camps." Here they were supposed to be reformed by hard labor and Communist indoctrination. Some served only days and others up to thirteen years! While there was no large-scale bloodbath immediately following the Communist takeover, Vietnam suffered a slow and painful bleeding as many thousands died out of sight in wretched camps of mistreatment and deprivation.[19]

What happened to churches and Christians during these dark days? Some key insights here come from the reflection of church leaders who themselves suffered greatly.

Hearts and Minds

During the first year after the end of the war, the northern victors allowed the southern Viet Cong to have a lot of say in operational control. The Viet Cong used a gentle policy of trying to win hearts and minds, including a fairly open policy toward religion and religious people. This policy was said to guarantee religious freedom—freedom to worship, respect for religious buildings, and the right of people to share their religion and to operate their schools. Religious believers were guaranteed all the rights of citizens. The policy guaranteed no persecution nor discrimination based on religion.

---

19 For a gripping first-person account of life in a "reeducation camp" see Doan Van Toai's in *The Vietnamese Gulag*.

Religious leaders were even invited to seek election to be the people's representatives. Catholic Father Chan Tin did run and win, but the outspoken priest did not last long in an office which required quiet obeisance.

Churches were allowed to continue public worship (exceptions concerning Montagnards are described below). Yet church attendance dropped considerably, especially in churches whose leaders had fled. The ECVN(S) was allowed to hold its annual general meeting, and the Bible school in Nhatrang remained open for the 1975–1976 school term. The Bible Society was allowed to sell its remaining stock but with cumbersome restrictions.

Nevertheless, trouble was in the air. The smaller denominations that had been heavily dependent on missionaries and were left with weak infrastructure dissolved. Their members who remained faithful identified with the ECVN(S). Military chaplains of the ECVN(S) were sentenced to very long terms of prison and reeducation. Two chaplains, the Reverend Nam and the Reverend Thang, would die in state custody.

With strong backing of the authorities, a lay Christian, Mr. Nguyen Thanh Long, began to pressure church organizations to form a "United Protestant Church." He used his government-granted authority to confiscate some expensive church properties in Saigon and transfer them to the government. But this government-backed church unity project collapsed when Mr. Long died suddenly and unexpectedly.

During this early period, the authorities completely dissolved the ethnic minority church districts of the ECVN(S) in the Central Highlands. They also forbade members of ethnic Vietnamese churches to tithe and support their pastors.

With official reunification of the two Vietnams in 1976, the northern victors had sufficient power to rule the south. They marginalized the southern Viet Cong and revealed their real face toward religion. The promises of the Viet Cong policy on respecting religions were discarded. Real pressure began. The much larger ECVN(S) was encouraged to join the ECVN(N). It declined because it had discovered that some ECVN(N) leaders had fallen under government control.

Sifting and Purification

It was now a time of sifting and purification. Those without genuine trust in God, including pastors, became immobilized by fear. Some church members fell away, returning to their previous way of living. Some Christians were so fearful that they hid or discarded their Bibles and anything else that might identify them.

Many young Christians became deeply discouraged at the weakness of ECVN(S) leaders in showing the way. They formed several underground fellowships to keep the faith and encourage one another. Authorities began to interfere directly in church leadership affairs, refusing to deal with leaders they called "bad elements" because they could not manipulate them. They also closed the Bible school at Nhatrang, confiscated the property, and turned the large seaside campus into a rest house for government labor unions.

Repression started in earnest. Protestant churches along with other religious bodies suffered the confiscation of all social institutions—schools, orphanages, medical clinics, and hospitals among them. Communist ideology considers religion a useless social vestige that will fall away as altruistic socialism provides all that people need. But in practice communism helps make sure that churches are useless by making it impossible for churches to minister to society. The valuable social ministries of Catholics and Protestants in Vietnamese society, which were large and widespread in both cases, were stopped overnight, sacrificed on the altar of ideology.

In the case of Protestants, some three hundred properties were seized. Today, thirty-five years later, few minor settlements have been offered, and the ECVN(S) is still contesting some 265 confiscated properties. The authorities now say it is too late.

Reasonable requests by the ECVN(S) after the change in government were routinely denied by the government because they considered it an illegal body. For example, for twenty-five years churches were not allowed to hold annual meetings in local churches, or at the district and national level. This completely disrupted normal church life.

Montagnard Christians suffered the worst mistreatment. About three hundred ethnic minority churches were closed, and all communal worship and other Christian activity ceased during these dark years. If Christians worshiped, they did so in the secrecy of their own homes. But even there they felt watched.

Because some Montagnards continued their resistance to the Communist victory after 1975 and because of some earlier Protestant involvement in FULRO's independence aspirations, at least two hundred Protestant pastors and leaders were rounded up and imprisoned. They not only suffered deep deprivation, but many were physically mistreated. Pastor Y Ngue, a prominent Ede tribal leader, was permanently crippled by brutal beatings during his imprisonment. A number died in prison camps. Survivors were not released until 1981.

The decision to ease up a little and to free Montagnard pastors was later regretted by some hardliners, but little by little Christians began to surface and seek each other out. They soon resumed meeting in small home groups, but always assigned a lookout.

"Only a Little Woman"

A remarkable and telling story surrounds the diminutive Mrs. Diep Thi Do, wife of Rev. Dang Van Sung. Since 1953 she and her husband had served as Vietnamese missionaries to the Stieng minority in Binh Phuoc province.

Missionaries Pastor and Mrs. Sung at their marriage.

Her husband was captured during a major Communist offensive in this area a couple of months before final Communist victory in April 1975. Missionary Sung was never heard from again. His widow hunkered down for six years, not daring any contact with Stieng Christians. She could only pray.

In 1981, emerging from the deep underground during the darkest years, she encountered some very discouraged Stieng Christians in the market. When they recognized her, they begged her to again be their pastor and missionary. After years without, they longed deeply for fellowship and for communal worship. She experienced this encounter as a strong call from God. From that time on she courageously called the Stieng back into church groups. Many times hostile authorities blocked her. She said, "With God's help, I stared them down!"

She bravely went throughout the Stieng region, fearlessly doing battle with government authorities to reopen closed churches in the 1980s and 1990s, long before the current thaw in government attitudes toward religion. She presided over the construction of the largest church building in Vietnam in Phuoc Long, seating two thousand people. At the time of her death in January 2008, she was constructing a three-story school for Stieng young people.

"Bishop" Mrs. Sung presides over a communion service for hundreds of Stieng believers.

Although the ECVN(S) does not ordain women, she performed all pastoral functions—marrying, burying, appointing leaders, and administering the sacraments. Her bravery and her spiritual authority ensured that no one ever challenged her operating essentially as a bishop! She said matter-of-factly, "I just had to do everything." Church leaders, who had developed a special category for her, simply shrugged and said, "Oh, that's Mrs. Sung."

She described herself as "only a little woman." But her faith and trust in God made her a giant in the lives of thousands of the Stieng Christians she had served for fifty-five years! More than four thousand came to attend her funeral and celebrate her life when she died at age eighty-four in 2008.

Blessing and Renewal in Hard Times

In the early 1980s, following a time of sifting and purification, God visited some churches in Saigon with unanticipated blessing and revival. Those who experienced this unusual time say that God used many means, including children, to convict Christians and their leaders of their lack of faith and courage during and immediately after the fear-filled Communist takeover.

Longing for God's power in the midst of their oppression, Christians in many places in Vietnam began to organize Bible studies, fasting, and prayer. Witnessing and evangelism were resumed and new believers were added to the church. The radically changed lives of new believers attracted nonbelievers to the faith. God visited His people with miracles of healing and deliverance from evil spirits, especially among the Montagnards. Many returned from long, harsh sentences in prisons and reeducation camps with a strengthened faith in God that they shared with family and friends.

The Tran Cao Van church in central Saigon experienced an unusual revival beginning in 1978. It ended in 1983, in a manner of speaking, with the arrest and long imprisonment of Pastor Ho Hieu Ha.

Pastor Ha and his wife had served as missionaries to the Mnong tribal people in the Central Highlands before the Communist victory. They were forced to flee to Saigon during the final days of fighting. There they were appointed to pastor a new Vietnamese congregation in the spacious Tran Cao Van church building, which had long served as an international church. It belonged legally to the ECVN(S) but was empty as all foreigners had left.

Pastor Ha testified that he was also overcome by fear in the early days after the Communist takeover. He began to pray earnestly for renewal and for courage. He also called others to regular early morning prayer. During one prayer event he experienced a sudden and miraculous deliverance from fear. The intense prayer times continued and began to attract more and more people. Pastor Ha, now endowed with godly courage, began to preach bold and clear evangelistic messages. From 1978–1983 the church recorded an average of a thousand new believers a year, many of whom were also baptized.

In December of 1983, unable to tolerate this unusual demonstration of vigorous Christian faith, authorities arrested Pastor Ha, closed the church, and confiscated the property. They also arrested Pastor Nguyen Huu Cuong and Le Thien Dung who were having a similarly successful ministry to students at the An Dong church across town. The three men would spend more than six years in prison. After strong international advocacy, which included the elder President Bush, they were finally offered release on condition of accepting exile to the US within twenty-four hours of being released. Not wanting to leave their homeland, they resisted this offer for a year before finally accepting in January 1990.

Thrown out of her home, Pastor Ha's courageous wife was obliged for a time to live with her children on an exposed balcony during the rainy season. She blessed and encouraged many by some remarkable "letters from a balcony" in which she praised God for His blessings and sustaining power, even in her desperate circumstances. Not surprisingly, the effect of closing these two thriving churches was to spread their spiritual fervor to many other places.

During this time some emboldened Christian leaders secretly printed badly needed Bibles, hymnals, and other Christian materials. Some renewed pastors and lay people volunteered to go from place to place, wherever asked, to preach, teach, and train. Christians began to worship in small groups in private homes, each using the gifts that God had given them—foreshadowing a house church movement to come.

"The Girl in the Picture"

One person who met God during the revival at Tran Cao Van would become world famous. She is Phan Thi Kim Phuc, better known as "the napalm girl," or Kim Phuc to her friends.

The sight of the little girl running naked and screaming from out of a napalm fireball was captured by Vietnamese cameraman Nick Ut on June 8, 1972. For many it became the most indelible image of the Vietnam War. Some believe it helped stop the war.

Much of Kim Phuc's incredible story is captivatingly told in the book *The Girl in the Picture* by best-selling author Denise Chong (1999). But here is some of "the rest of the story."

Kim Phuc's "coming out" in North America was at the Vietnam War Memorial in Washington, DC, in 1996. She had defected to Canada in 1992 but had decided to lie low because of the extreme stress that she had been put under in Vietnam, where the government had constantly used her as a propaganda tool. It had wearied her to the point of complete exhaustion, precluding any kind of a normal life.

After her speech at the memorial and her stunning on-the-spot forgiveness of the US officer who approached her there, claiming he had been complicit in the bombing that had injured her, there was no more hiding or lying low for Kim!

The first news I heard about her included the fact that she had become a devout Christian in Vietnam. I had a very strong sense that I was somehow personally connected. Hours later I learned the name of the pastor who had led her to faith and the one who had baptized her. One had been a seminary student of mine and the other was my Vietnamese spiritual godfather!

In late 1996 I was preparing to host the 10th General Assembly of the World Evangelical Fellowship (WEF) in Abbotsford, British Columbia, Canada. I asked

Kim if she would give her testimony at the assembly in May 1997. She accepted, and we prepared for the big night.

The Canadian Broadcasting Corporation (CBC) had created a wonderful hour-long documentary on her life, which was broadcast in the fall of 1996. It included a powerful movie clip of the moments before the famous photo was snapped. A movie photographer had also been with Nick Ut when he shot his Pulitzer prize-winning still picture of the "napalm girl."

On the evening of the event, two thousand people packed into Central Heights Church. The sanctuary was darkened. On a huge screen we projected the first half minute of the CBC documentary at full volume! War planes screamed downward, bombs dropping and exploding behind some trees into fiery red flames. Terrified children came running out of black smoke directly toward the camera, which had focused on little Kim. We froze the frame when it showed the top half of Kim, her face screaming with pain and terror. Then a spotlight shone on stage door right. I walked out with Kim on my arm, took her to center stage and said, "Sisters and brothers, I have the honor of introducing you to Kim Phuc, the napalm girl. Hear her testimony in her own words." Yes, you could have heard a pin drop!

During her riveting story she told about a Christian friend who had invited her to the Tran Cao Van church. She was much attracted to the discussion about the meaning of life. She heard several powerful messages from Pastor Ha, messages she says seemed prepared specifically for her. After one of them she was convicted of her need for God's mercy and placed her faith in Christ. A very bright and inquiring person, she grew rapidly in her new faith, finding in it a serenity that her frenzied external life denied her. Her worldview was forever altered. In December of 1983, just a year after Kim became a believer, Pastor Ha was arrested and imprisoned for six years. The church was permanently closed, and the property confiscated and turned to use by the Communist Youth League.

After Kim completed her story, I moved to center stage with her. I told her that Pastor Ha had been my student and asked her how long it had been since she had seen him. She thought for a moment and said, "Fifteen years." At that moment a spotlight moved to stage door left catching Pastor and Mrs. Ha moving toward us. After fifteen very eventful years, the three were reunited in front of the audience of two thousand! His arms around both women, Pastor Ha cried out to God in praise! Not a dry eye in the house!

After her conversion Kim remained caught in the Communist propaganda machine, which forever paraded her as victim. Interviews and "photo ops" for foreign journalists were unending. In 1985, thirteen years after her burning, one American reporter showed Kim the movie footage of the bombing. Yes, she knew the famous picture, but it was only after seeing the perspective of the movie that she truly understood why she had become a living symbol of the horror of war.

Vietnamese prime minister at the time, Pham Van Dong, took a special interest in Kim. He treated her like a beloved daughter. He invited her to his homes in Hanoi and Ho Chi Minh City for meals and visits several times. On one occasion she told the prime minister about how the incessant demands for interviews and photos wore her down and interrupted her dream of getting good education. He subsequently arranged for her to study in Cuba. During what she expected would be her final meeting with the prime minister, he listened politely as Kim clearly shared the gospel with him.

With no known Christians around her in Cuba, Kim struggled to nourish her faith. While in Cuba some of Kim's girlfriends tried to match her with an earnest fellow student, a North Vietnamese named Toan. Though he was a committed Communist and not a Christian, Kim prayed diligently. She believed God gave her permission to marry Toan, so after a short courtship they were married in the Vietnamese Embassy in Havana. Their government awarded them a honeymoon to Moscow! On the return to Cuba, their plane had to refuel in Gander, Newfoundland. Kim and Toan walked off the plane and applied for and were granted asylum. They settled in Toronto.

Kim and family at Christmas 2010. From left to right: Danielle (Kim's niece), Kim, husband Toan, and sons Steven and Thomas.

Toan became a believer within weeks of arriving in Canada. They both became very active in their church in Ajax, near Toronto. Kim and Toan have been blessed with two sons. Kim brought her parents to Canada in 1998 on tourist visas. She then asked me how to proceed to apply for permanent residence status for them. I said I did not know. "Never mind," she said, "I will use my famous." She did—and was successful.

Kim's mother, Nu, has been a huge help in looking after the boys as Kim is away on her many speaking appointments around the world. Since 1997 Kim has traveled the world as goodwill ambassador for UNESCO.

Kim's resilience and joy, in spite of continued physical difficulties with her burn scars, is amazing. Her life revolves around her faith in God. Her remarkable story gives her entrée to share the gospel regularly with princes and princesses, kings and queens, presidents and prime ministers, and dignitaries too numerous to mention. She considers her "misfortune" as God's preparation for this unprecedented ministry. Her signature statement says it all: "It was the fire of the bombs that burned my body. It was the skill of the doctors that mended my skin, but it took the power of God's love to heal my heart!"

Kim Phuc with son Thomas. Photo © Anne Bayin.

It all started when Kim encountered Christ in 1982 at the Tran Cao Van revival during Vietnam's "Dark Decade" following the Communist victory.

Manipulating the Church

When the authorities saw that the effects of their pressure on Christians were the precise opposite of their goal, they seemed to rethink their strategy. They eased up a bit and tried a second time to create a unified Protestant church.

In 1984, with the agreement of the ECVN(S) president, the Reverend Ong Van Huyen, Pastor Nguyen Van Quan emerged as the leader of a new committee, which agreed under government pressure to abolish the ECVN(S) constitution and prepare a new one. Most leaders believed this was another government attempt at creating a unified Protestant church under its control. This led quickly to much divisiveness in the church, involving both pastors and lay Christians. Many felt the leaders cooperating with the government were betraying them.

Doing the Necessary

When the enemy puts up a barrier, God's people often find a way around it.

The effective spiritual leadership of the ECVN(S) passed to the vice president, the Reverend Doan Van Mieng. He had long served as president but had been demoted to vice president by manipulation at the one post-Communist general assembly allowed by the authorities in 1976. Pastor Mieng believed the authorities were completely untrustworthy and for the most part declined to deal with them. He courageously did what he believed necessary to guard and preserve the church.

God used him in helping to reestablish and renew the Montagnard churches. Pastor Mieng had a high respect for and good relationships with tribal Christians, unlike many Vietnamese who tended to look down on them. His heart was broken at their extreme suffering.

With the Montagnard churches' organizational structure disbanded by the government, a way forward had to be found. Pastor Mieng encouraged the formation of provincial "prayer committees." These not only met secretly for prayer, but became the churches' communication and administration channel. These prayer committees also trained new leaders as best they could in very difficult circumstances and quietly planted new churches. Of necessity, Pastor Mieng authorized unordained pastors and even lay leaders to perform marriages, baptize people, and administer the sacraments.

The Communist victory proved a momentous event for Protestant Christians in Vietnam. Fear and confusion led to some falling away and retreat. Many came under intense repression and persecution. The faithful sought strength from God and were visited with revival and new courage. Leaders found creative ways to lead, teach, and grow their churches. This set the stage for significant future expansion.

The Revolution Deeply Disillusions

Paradise of the Blind and other novels

Vietnamese novelist Duong Thu Huong offers deep insights into Vietnamese culture and the growing disillusionment felt by millions following the success of the Communist revolution.[20]

Born in 1947, Huong served for nearly ten years in a propaganda troupe intended to buoy the troops on the front lines of the wars against the Americans and in 1979 against the Chinese. Her job was "to sing louder than the bombs" as well as to tend to the wounded and bury the dead. She knew hardship, danger, suffering, and great sacrifice firsthand. But the high hopes for the revolution were followed by even more suffering and deprivation, and exacerbated by the corruption and hypocrisy of Communist leaders. This translated soon into deep disillusionment.

Once the darling of the Party for some of her earlier propaganda work, she fell out of favor with the publication of her third novel, *Paradise of the Blind* (1993). The novel described the horrors and brutality of land reform in the mid-1950s under Ho Chi Minh during which many thousands of peasants lost their lives. This book scandalized Vietnam's Communist leaders and was removed from circulation. Communist Party Secretary Nguyen Linh fell to calling Huong a "dissident slut," an epithet she considered a badge of honor. Huong was expelled from the Party in a meeting of the cell in which she was a member, when she courageously cast the deciding vote against herself.

Huong was jailed and held in solitary confinement for seven months in 1991 when she was caught trying to smuggle *Novel Without a Name* to publishers abroad. This novel, set during the war, turned out to be the first in a trilogy. Her translator, Nina McPherson, quotes the young male narrator of the novel in one poignant section:

> Ten years ago we wanted to sing songs of glory. Anything was
> good for killing as long as it brought glory. But the war comes
> back to haunt the soldiers in dreams and hallucinations, in visions

---

20 A fascinating biography and bibliography of her works can be found at the website Wikivietlit under Duong Thu Huong. The author is Nina McPherson, the able English translator of some of Huong's novels. This section includes a selective summary of that posting. See References for website.

of walking vultures that remind him of villages razed to ash, strewn
with swollen corpses, of the gorges that swam with blood and
rotting flesh; of the stench of death, the buzzing of flies.
(McPherson n.d.)

The novelist is a master at evoking strong feelings, sounds, smells, and vivid
color. She crosses the line between real and surreal, and draws on traditional
Vietnamese fantasy conventions of storytelling in which the line between animate and inanimate is often blurred. Rocks and trees have souls which can
separate themselves from their hosts, and the hungry souls of dead soldiers
return to haunt the living (ibid.).

Huong added two post-war novels—*Memories of a Pure Spring* (2000) and
later the powerful *No Man's Land* (2005), her most tragic and acclaimed novel.
These novels, which have all undergone numerous reprintings in English and
French and a dozen other languages, remain banned in Vietnam. However, they
circulate widely, clandestinely.

The Sorrow of War

The Sorrow of War (1994), perhaps the best-known Vietnamese war novel, was
written by a North Vietnamese soldier and translated into English. Bao Ninh, the
author's pen name, was one of only ten survivors of five hundred youth of the
Glorious 27th Youth Brigade.

Parted by war from his youthful sweetheart, the protagonist, Kien, endures the
most horrific experiences in war. His unrequited love and the horrors of war are
repeatedly recalled in a nonlinear, surreal fashion, changing color each time.

The truly pathetic reality of the novel is that all the sacrifices of youth, love,
life, family, and tradition completely fail to deliver the promises that prompted
them. It seems Bao Ninh valiantly tries for some redemption in this exposé of
the realities of war. For its troubling message, the novel was banned for a time
in Vietnam. Unlike novelist Duong Thu Huong, Bao Ninh went silent after one
epic publication, apparently a result of official pressure and personal brokenness. To know something of the war from a foot soldier on the Communist
Vietnamese side, one cannot do better than read *The Sorrow of War*, told in a
very Vietnamese way. Various publishers have reprinted it numerous times in
several languages.

CHAPTER 7

Birth of the
House Church Movement

Contributing Factors

The tensions over leadership within the ECVN(S) in 1984 contributed to the birth of the house church movement just four years later. Some young and capable pastors lost confidence in some ECVN(S) leaders who openly courted government favor in the belief that this was the only way to keep the churches open. Such men were called "state enterprise" (*quoc doanh*) pastors. The young pastors certainly had no confidence in the pastor chosen to be the liaison with the government. This man had already proven himself treacherous, reporting to the authorities about one worker who was printing Bibles and Christian materials underground. That brother spent seven years in prison!

Another Saigon church that experienced strong growth and vigorous spiritual life in the 1980s was the Tuy Ly Vuong congregation, led by Pastor Dinh Thien Tu. So many people were being added that even with multiple services it was bursting at the seams. Home groups were formed as well to accommodate the growth.

Some very cautious ECVN(S) leaders feared the activities at Tuy Ly Vuong would attract the kind of attention that prompted the government to arrest the pastors and close the Tran Cao Van and An Dong congregations in 1983. Moreover, this congregation and some others were exhibiting signs that Pentecostal and charismatic ideas and worship styles had influenced them. The Assemblies of God had introduced Pentecostal doctrine and practices to Vietnam in the early 1970s, and an influential French charismatic missionary had been among the first to visit Vietnam when the door cracked open in 1986. That was when Vietnam initiated its Doi Moi policy, which copied the former Soviet Union's *perestroika* ("reform") idea, but not the *glasnost* ("openness") one.

Vietnam's major reform was to largely replace Marxist economic approach with a market economy. It decidedly did not move toward political openness.

In matters Pentecostal or charismatic (Vietnamese Christians do not distinguish the two), the ECVN(S) was much more conservative than its founding C&MA mission. C&MA founder, Dr. A. B. Simpson, preached a "seek not, forbid not" policy toward charismatic gifts. A combination of factors, including government pressure, caused the ECVN(S) to expel Pastor Tu in 1988 for insubordination. Many in his thriving church stayed with their strong leader. The meetings already going on in many homes made for an instant house church network. It came to be called the Christian Fellowship Church and became, for a time, the largest house church group.

Within the same year, three other ECVN(S) pastors—Vo Van Lac, Tran Mai, and Tran Dinh Ai—were put on probation and then expelled from the ECVN(S) for, among other things, "tolerating and practicing speaking in tongues." Pastor Lac's group came to be called the Full Gospel Church and later developed a relationship with the international Foursquare Church. Pastor Ai reconnected with the Assemblies of God which he had been part of prior to 1975, and Pastor Mai's group was called the Inter-Evangelistic Movement. It was not long before some foreign organizations began generously supporting factions of these first four house church groups, creating ever more house church organizations. Since the early house church leaders originated from the ECVN(S), not surprisingly there were tensions between some ECVN(S) leaders and the new groups.

The first house church leaders also credit the prayer movement of the early 1980s for revival in ECVN(S) churches. Many agreed that the church was in a stagnant and fearful condition. Spiritual life and fervor had declined. Christians felt they had not been prepared for life under communism. They longed for renewal and spiritual power. However, the leaders did not anticipate that being expelled was the way their prayer would be answered.

But once out on their own, the fledgling house churches developed rapidly. Many people were attracted to their evangelistically bold leaders. The joyful worship of their fellowships and evidence of the Holy Spirit's power in witness, miracles, and worship soon led to rapid growth.

The movement's leaders, especially Pastor Tu, also traced the initial rapid house church growth to a course they had taken in their ECVN(S) training during 1972 and 1973. A missionary and a pastor had returned from studying church growth at Fuller Seminary's School of World Mission. They taught a course in church growth principles to Vietnamese seminarians and pastors. In retrospect, it seems the lasting impact of the course was that it introduced those who studied it to various effective church models and methods of church planting. Vietnam had long been dominated by only one quite hierarchical and building-based model. This exposure gave them other models and the freedom of flexibility and experimenting so necessary to "doing church" in a repressive situation. Importantly, it freed them from the idea that a church building was required for congregational life, thereby making rapid expansion possible.

Explosive Start

The growth of the four original house church organizations was explosive in their first ten years, but then it slowed somewhat in the late 1990s. By 2009 there were an estimated 250,000 Christians in at least 2,500 home-based groups belonging to house church organizations. As well, the original number of four house church organizations exploded to seventy!

Today these organizations range from single congregations to ones that have hundreds of congregations. Some have become connected to international denominations such as the Assemblies of God, Nazarenes, Methodists, Mennonites, and Presbyterians. Others are independent, though these also receive support from overseas agencies. The largest house church groups claim they have twenty-five to thirty thousand believers. In the beginning, house churches were primarily an urban phenomenon; they remain strong in the cities today. One recent survey showed that house church worshipers in greater Ho Chi Minh City on a given Sunday number well over thirty thousand, significantly more than the estimated twenty-two thousand who worship in churches of the historic ECVN(S).

Several factors led to the multiplication from four to seventy house church organizations over the course of two decades. People representing organizations and churches from a number of Asian countries, as well as from North America, Europe, and Australia, began going to Vietnam in the 1990s. One researcher has a list of nearly five hundred evangelical organizations, from very small to large as well as overseas Vietnamese groups, that reported they had something going in Vietnam. A fair number of them wanted their own church organization, and some contributed to the splitting of house church groups by offering financial incentives to recruit existing workers. Some argued that having many different organizations was actually helpful in that it made it harder for repressive authorities to keep track.

Overseas financial assistance came to be commonly used to support church workers. These were often called "missionaries, church planters, or evangelists" to indicate an outreach function. But, in fact, permanent pastors of congregations also came to be supported in this way—even some who had managed well without it for many years. This practice conflicted with the historic three-self principles which prevailed during the first fifty years of Protestant mission in Vietnam. This methodology held that indigenous churches, their limited resources notwithstanding, would be healthier and growth more sustainable if congregations supported themselves even in early stages of development.

There came a time when the house churches themselves realized that the continual splitting and starting of new groups, often because of too easily available foreign money, was not a healthy reflection of the Christian gospel. With encouragement from the World Evangelical Alliance and the Vietnam World Christian Fellowship (an organization of overseas Vietnamese churches and leaders), a number of southern-based house churches got together in the mid-1990s to form the Vietnam Evangelical Fellowship (of house churches). Today VEF includes twenty-nine southern-based house church groups and works effectively in some joint projects. In 2009 a number of house churches in Hanoi and other parts of the north formed the Hanoi Christian Fellowship. Meanwhile, some other house church groups remain independent and unconnected.

The ECVN(S) and ethnic minority churches in the northwest related to the ECVN(N) also grew rapidly during this time by planting and adding many house churches. Without permission and adequate funds to build chapels and churches, Christian believers found house churches to be the only option. I point this out to underline that the house church model is not confined to the many house church organizations. It is a response to political, social, and economic realities.

A House Church in the City

It's 9:00 a.m. on a Sunday morning in Ho Chi Minh City. The day is heating up. People wearing their best clothes make their way up three flights of stairs to the small apartment of Mr. and Mrs. Nguyen in a residential area of the city. Eighteen people overfill the main room, sitting on the furniture and the floor. The meeting begins. Two young people, one with a guitar, lead in loud and joyful singing. A Westerner would recognize some familiar praise song tunes, but not other traditional Vietnamese ones.

Next, a woman about forty years of age directs the group in a time of prayer. Those present are invited to share their concerns. There is no holding back. Several have lost work and need a job. Two have sick children. One young woman is waiting for news about whether she will be accepted to a university. Another woman is being badly treated by her husband who is not a Christian. The names of family members and others who are not believers are mentioned for prayer. Then eight people—including men, women, and young people—lead in earnest, intense prayer for twenty minutes.

After an offering box is passed around, a young pastor in his thirties, who will do this twice more before the day is out, opens the Bible to 1 Peter 4 and speaks for half an hour on verses 12–19, beginning with "Do not be surprised at the painful trial you are suffering." When he is done, several respond in prayer. After the pastor gives a benediction, some leave promptly, while a few remain, drinking tea supplied by Mrs. Nguyen and visiting quietly before slipping off.

CHAPTER 8

The Remarkable
Hmong People Movement

A House Church in the Mountains

High in the mountains of northwest Vietnam's Lai Chau province lies Muong Te district. There are dozens of villages, each a loose pattern of ten to twenty wood-and-thatch houses scattered by the dictates of the rough terrain. At least fifty villages of ethnic minority Hmong in this district have congregations which meet in homes. Let's look at one.

Mr. Vang, a respected elder, and his wife have offered their house as a meeting place. The main room of the attractive house has a clean, smooth earthen floor, containing a large family-bed platform and a few plastic chairs. People begin arriving midmorning; soon about thirty men and a few women fill the main room of the house. Some forty others, many of them women carrying or towing small children, gather around the open windows and the door. The women are wearing intricately designed costumes of red and black.

When it seems most have arrived, a middle-aged man who serves as the church leader begins the service. He became a believer eleven years earlier by hearing a Far East Broadcasting Company gospel program in his own language. He has been interrogated often and imprisoned several times for his Christian faith. His opening prayer includes the petition, "Dear Lord, do not let the authorities disturb us as we worship today." This is followed by vigorous singing led by some young people.

The leader then directs a time of prayer. The needs expressed are basic and clear. "Ask the Lord to heal my sick mother." "Pray the Lord will protect my husband who was called by the officials for an 'interview' about why he is Christian." "Ask God that our sow will give birth to healthy piglets. Without this we will go hungry." "Pray for us brothers who will this week go to a remote village to share the gospel. Even though this is forbidden by the authorities, we must go!"

The church leader then opens his Hmong Bible, which the authorities consider illegal. Though there are some 350,000 Hmong Christians in Vietnam, the authorities have not allowed a single Hmong-language Bible to be officially printed in Vietnam. But a number of Christians are carrying small, illegal Bibles and intently follow the reading. They have taught themselves to read by using it. The message is from 2 Timothy 1:8—"join with me in suffering for the gospel, by the power of God." In conclusion people respond in prayer. Small groups visit for a while and then slowly drift off to their own homes. The young people stay for a meeting of their own.

The Gospel by Radio

The largest movement to Protestant Christian faith in Vietnam started in a most unusual way. Following the fall of Vietnam, Laos, and Cambodia to communism in 1975, one ministry that could continue was radio broadcasting. In the case of ethnic minority languages such as Koho, Ede, and Jarai, programs were even expanded. They often included Bible reading as it was known most Scriptures had been lost or destroyed. Radio was one way to encourage and strengthen these groups. Refugee pastors and sometimes missionaries became the radio voices. The Far East Broadcasting Company (FEBC), with headquarters in the Philippines and transmitters strategically positioned elsewhere as well, was the main broadcaster of such programs.

Blue Hmong women. Hmong are distinguished by colors used in their traditional costumes—such as Blue Hmong, Black Hmong, White Hmong, and Flowery Hmong. Importantly, these designations also indicate a dialect difference.

A Hmong pastor, who had fled communism in Laos, prepared gospel broadcasts at his home in California using the radio name of John Lee. These were broadcast to reach Hmong people living not only in Laos but in Vietnam, China, Burma, and Thailand. John Lee was a gifted preacher, but like many other broadcasters, he honestly wondered about the scope and effectiveness of the radio medium.

A Black Hmong extended family. A movement to Christian faith has just recently begun among the Black Hmong in Vietnam.

Part of his sign-off on the broadcasts included an invitation to write a response to FEBC. Beginning in 1987 Pastor Lee began receiving letters from Vietnam. By 1989 these had turned into a deluge—more than FEBC had ever received from anywhere before! The writers of these letters told Lee that they had accepted Christ and asked for more information and guidance. There were thousands!

In those days it was impossible to visit the new followers and help them on their way. What happened in the high mountains during those early days later came to light. The information came from Hmong leaders who subsequently shared their story with the ECVN(N), a church they identified with. More information came from some who sadly had to flee their country.

The story of the Hmong movement to Christ is one full of New Testament hardship and suffering but also blessing. This can be illustrated in the life of one courageous man who fled Vietnam in 2005 after sixteen years of persecution. TAT, as we will call him, is one of the pioneers of the Hmong church now numbering some 350,000!

The Story of One

Following a daring escape from Vietnam through Laos, TAT and family
arrived in Thailand in 2005. They were classified as bona fide refugees by
the United Nations High Commission for Refugees (UNHCR). But while
waiting for US immigration processing, he and family were arrested by Thai
immigration authorities and forced to spend a year in the sweltering Suan
Plu Immigration Detention Center in Bangkok. There he wrote his incredible story, which I quote at some length because it is so representative of what
happened to the Hmong Christian leaders.[21]

*Because of the traditional animistic beliefs of our people who lived in the mountains,
I was very superstitious. When we had sickness in our household we invited shamans to
come and make offerings to the spirits and to the dead so that we could get well. But by so
doing we were often harmed by the spirits. Also, I was taught to be careful of many things
to escape calamity, such as stopping toads or snakes from entering my home because those
species were believed to bring bad luck to the house. Even a dog's climbing to the roof of the
house was considered to be a sign of calamity. I had no moment of contentment, only confusion and anxiety. I could not sleep or eat well.*

*In that time of confusion, I had a chance to hear Source of Life Radio and came to
realize that I needed to trust in God. I had two brothers who also loved to listen to this
program. I remember how eagerly we discussed what we had heard. We concluded ancestor worship and other beliefs did not help us much. So we became Christians on August 5,
1989. After that, I prayed asking that no demon or spirit would possess my family, and
God answered my prayers.*

TAT not only became a believer but a zealous and brave evangelist.
His story lists sixteen separate arrests and imprisonments between 1989 and
2005, when he finally fled. The prison internments lasted from a few days to
three years. They were accompanied by unimaginable punishment and torture. Among them was hard labor in cutting wood or breaking hard soil. On
one occasion he left a hoe in the field.

*On the way back, some guards threw me to the ground and struck me repeatedly with
that heavy piece of wood. This beating on my lower back was extremely painful, and I
urinated blood.*

---

21 This information is from my translation of a lengthy testimony written by TAT in his ap-
    peal for asylum.

In another case, TAT and three other evangelists were arrested at a border post and imprisoned for six weeks.

We were severely beaten and made to sleep without blankets in the cold winter weather. They did not even allow us to use our sandals or backpacks as pillows. Our legs were locked in metal shackles, and we lay shivering on the cold cement floor.

Often persecution was brought to the villages where Christians lived.

Many officials came and acted like barbarians. Then they demanded each family give them two chickens and two liters of rice wine. They scattered a layer of sharp pebbles on the road surface and ordered us to kneel on it. Then they killed the chickens and forced us to drink chicken blood and pressured us to curse God and promise to be loyal to the Communist Party.

In the mid-1990s TAT heard John Lee mention on the radio a Protestant church in Hanoi. He was determined to try to make a connection.

We longed to have someone to teach us about Christianity. So we decided to go to Hanoi and find the church. We hoped that some pastors there could help us so we would not be so badly persecuted. Because the government forbade us to leave our villages, we stole away secretly at night, eventually reaching Hanoi. We first found a Catholic church. We asked the Catholics about a Protestant church but they did not reply. The Catholics did help us to make a petition about the beatings and persecution we had suffered and sent it to the central government. But to our surprise, they also notified the local government of our province, including our thirteen names! We were quite certain they would arrest all of us if we went back. So, we sent two men back home to test the situation. Immediately they were put into prison.

Then we went to a believer named Ho at Sung Ma and asked him to go to Laos to inquire about the location of the Protestant church in Hanoi. In Laos he met the superintendent of the Lao church and got the address of the Protestant church in Hanoi. After nine days he returned and told us the address. Mr. Ho also brought us a Hmong Bible. I was overjoyed to read it. Others asked me to teach them the Bible, which I did. I also taught them to read the Hmong language.

We returned to Hanoi and found the church. Pastor Thu and his assistant Vinh did not believe that there were Hmong believers. As a test, they asked us to sing a hymn, which we did forthwith. Then the pastors accepted that we were true believers. Through this, God's Holy Spirit strengthened us, and we went on our way home encouraged.

Three times TAT and his colleagues were arrested for transporting Bibles. These arrests and others were accompanied by heavy fines they could only pay by borrowing money. TAT's final imprisonment convinced him there was little future for him in Vietnam.

I was taken at night to a room and the door was locked. They interrogated me asking, "Do you know why you were imprisoned?" I said because I was a Christian. They agreed. They asked, "Do you know the laws of the prison?" I said I did not. They answered, "We will teach you here and now." The four laws of prison were:

You must obey promptly.

You are not allowed to see.

You are not allowed to know.

You are not allowed to hear.

They said I was obliged to carry these laws with me wherever I went. I said I would remember them in my heart. They said, no, they would bang them into my head first. They ordered, "Turn your face to the wall and remember this." Then they slammed my head against the wall ten times and I passed out. I had severe pain in my head and felt I would die. They said now I would remember these four things forever.

Next they forced me to kneel down, and then they kicked me hard in the chest until I passed out. I must have looked as if I were dead so, they splashed cold water on me, soaking me and bringing me to.

Then they said they would box my ears so I would understand what they were saying. They forced me to lie on one side and then took a hard sandal and hit it three times on my ear. Then they turned me over and hit my other ear. I could not hear anything for over two weeks and still have hearing problems.

After that, two of them sat on me. They trussed my arms and my legs so that I could not move. Then they used a torch to singe the hair on my body and began to scrape my skin like you do when you are butchering a pig. They singed and scraped, singed and scraped.

Then they took the burning torch and hit my private part numerous times. Next they took a hot cinder from the torch and wrote on my stomach and also pressed it on my private part. I was unable to urinate normally for a long time.

TAT and some colleagues who could write sent many letters of complaint to the prime minister, but nothing was addressed. TAT concluded, "All the government did was to investigate where the petitions came from and then punish the people who wrote them." Finally TAT came to the end of his endurance.

On February 17, 2005, I received an arrest warrant signed by Mr. Pham Van De, deputy chief of the district police. I decided to hide and rightly so. They sent more arrest warrants to my house and recruited people to hunt me. Sometimes at night I sneaked home to hug my children. They cried asking me, "Why does it take you so long to go looking for the buffalo?" Then I cried since I could not give them an answer. I rushed back to the forest after warning my children not to tell anyone that they had seen me. Though they were still young, they knew that the policemen wanted to arrest me. I was distraught after so many years of being hounded. I could not care for my family. I could not even have one peaceful sleep. I fled to Laos, praying my family would follow.

In his appeal for asylum, TAT wrote as follows:

After sixteen years of such treatment simply because I am a Christian believer, I could take it no longer. None of the new laws of freedom of religion that we heard about from Hanoi had any positive effect for our Hmong people. We were fined, persecuted, imprisoned, tortured, and humiliated as if we were not human. I deeply regret we had no choice but to leave our home and possessions and flee in search of security and freedom.

In spite of all of this mistreatment, TAT remained a faithful evangelist and witness for sixteen years, sharing the gospel widely and planting many churches in several provinces. He carried the gospel he heard by radio to the mountains. "How beautiful on the mountains are the feet of those who bring good news" (Isa 52:7). His experiences were repeated in the lives of many others. Dozens of leaders spent long periods in harsh prisons. Some died in prison. Some were killed by other means in large government prisons. Many thousands of Christians have been heavily pressured to sign documents recanting their faith. But still new people believe, the church grows, and Hmong are also taking the gospel to other ethnic groups!

"Unregulated Migration"

"Unregulated migration" was another sin that Hmong Christians were accused of by authorities. The situation for Christians was so harsh in the Northwest Mountainous Region that they began to look for easier places in Vietnam to live. In 1996 an indigenous mission working with the Hmong helped a key leader, who had suffered greatly and was being threatened with death, to move to the Central Highlands in southern Vietnam. He was actually "adopted" by Montagnard Christians, given a new name, a house, and some land. Later his family was brought to join him. This move became a precursor to a large migration of Hmong traveling eight hundred miles from the northern mountains to the Central Highlands. Government figures say there are now more than thirty-seven thousand who have "self-migrated" to the Central Highlands and that the vast majority are Christians.[22]

For the hope of less persecution, they abandoned homes and fields. But often they encountered new and unforeseen hardships. These migrants had no choice but to settle on poor, undeveloped land. But they worked diligently to make something out of it. Then, often, just when they were ready to harvest their first crops, Vietnamese authorities announced their settlements illegal and drove them from their new villages, seizing the crops and land for themselves!

"Don't Follow the Bad People"

Just praying to the Lord produces nothing. Only if you work will you eat.

In the early 2000s the Vietnamese government circulated blatantly anti-Christian propaganda booklets, often with both Vietnamese and Hmong text. One such booklet published in 2001 had a large snake on the cover and was not so subtly titled *Don't Believe the Snake Poison Words*.

Another published in 2004 was named *Don't Follow the Bad People*, referring to Christians. It was augmented with illustrations which either falsely pitted Christianity against local culture or caricatured Christian beliefs and practices as in this illustration.

Modest Improvements

Ironically, just as TAT fled Vietnam, things began to improve a little. Based on the new religion legislation of 2004–2005, the ECVN(N) tried to register with the government the hundreds of Hmong congregations it had accepted into membership. But after submitting five hundred registration applications,

---

22   This figure is from the 2008 version of a Vietnamese-language, internal government training manual prepared by the Government Bureau of Religious Affairs to train religion personnel on how to manage Protestant churches.

the ECVN(N) was told by government officials to stop. In any event none were approved until late 2006. It took the government until the end of 2009 to register 160 congregations, about 15 percent of the one thousand plus churches.

These registrations made some congregations legal, but local authorities also misused them. Contrary to religion laws, the officials required lists of Christians' names or imposed time limitations on how long the registrations last. The registrations were also sometimes used to exclude people and prevent impossible-to-foresee church activities not explicitly listed on the registration applications.

Hmong Church Challenges

The training of Hmong church leaders is a most critical need. Underground programs have long been the main means. They are still much needed even though since 2007 the ECVN(N) has been allowed to offer short trainings for leaders of the limited number of registered groups.

The lack of training and minimal training of Hmong leaders, largely because of government restrictions, contributes much to strong tensions with the government. A poorly understood faith is a major handicap for Christians in a context where the state ideology, the culture, the society, and the family suspect and fear a new religion.

The Hmong are still without a legal Bible. Authorities have refused to allow printing in the Romanized Hmong script through which many thousands of Christian Hmong have become literate. They say they will allow a printing, but it is an obscure script developed by a Vietnamese linguist during Ho Chi Minh's time that no one can read. Leaders believe this is just another attempt to try to slow Christian development.

Cults, such as the dangerous Eastern Lightening, and political movements work hard to infiltrate the undertrained Hmong churches and are sometimes successful. Vietnamese authorities for a time willfully confused Christianity with a historic Hmong myth about Vang Chu, a messiah-like figure who would come to unite and rescue the Hmong. The Vietnamese thus accused Hmong Christians of being a divisive political threat.

In another strategy, authorities abandoned the traditional Marxist view that all religions are superstition and should be discarded. They began promoting the "good and beautiful" ancient traditions and beliefs of the Hmong, including ancestor worship, as an antidote to rapidly growing Christianity. Now, in place of government "work sessions" to turn back Christianity, authorities reward family members who still follow traditional beliefs, and encourage shamans to apply immense social pressure on Christians to recant.

The need for basic Christian training for the many new Hmong believers is a constant challenge. Because of the sheer numbers of new Christians, the best efforts of the small ECVN(N) could not suffice. Discreet visits by teachers from abroad played a key part in filling the gap. And, as early as the mid-1990s some southern-based house church organizations went north to connect with Hmong congregations offering teaching and affiliation with their group. Unfortunately, these activities sometime proved competitive and divisive. Hmong Christians for the most part, saw themselves as belonging to one body.

Having grown from zero Christians twenty years ago to making up a full quarter of all of Vietnam's Protestants, the Hmong remain the group most vulnerable to religious repression. But no efforts of the state have been able to stop the progress of God's kingdom among this ethnic minority.

CHAPTER 9

The Vietnamese Diaspora

Since the 1975 Communist victory in Vietnam, four waves of Vietnamese emigrants have gone abroad. The first wave included the so-called evacuees, who were taken by Americans on planes and ships right at the fall. The second wave is the "boat people," who escaped southern Vietnam after the fall. Thousands from the north joined them beginning in 1980. Third were the thousands who went abroad as guest workers from the north to the Soviet Union and Eastern Bloc countries until the collapse of communism there. And finally, beginning in the late 1990s to the present, are the tens of thousands of Vietnamese, including ethnic minorities, who have gone to work in Malaysia, South Korea, Taiwan, and other countries even further away. These four movements have all had a major impact on the kingdom of God in Vietnam.

Right after my evacuation from Vietnam with the last Canadians on April 24, 1975, the C&MA assigned me to the Pacific island of Guam. Here I led a dozen missionaries who served as interpreters and troubleshooters for the US military, which transported 150,000 Vietnamese by planes and ships to Guam. We missionaries also served as chaplains, gathering Christians for worship and providing them with Bibles and songbooks. We also shared the gospel and distributed Christian literature to others (Cowles 1976, 121–34).

The evacuees were promptly sent from Guam to US military bases on the mainland for immigration processing. The C&MA and Southern Baptists assigned missionaries to bases such as Fort Chaffee, Arkansas and Camp Pendleton, California. Here missionaries served not only to help with government processing but also, as missionaries in Guam had done, they acted as chaplains, evangelists, and encouragers to people who had left everything behind. Significant numbers were led to faith.

The next wave of emigration was the boat people. The first ones embarked from the conquered South, but beginning in 1980 large numbers also left the North, especially from the port city of Hai Phong. It is believed thousands perished in the South China Sea. Many were lost in small, unseaworthy boats in heavy weather. Countless others perished at the hands of cruel pirates in the South China Sea and the Gulf of Siam. Yet many thousands who left by sea made it safely to Thailand, Malaysia, the Philippines, Indonesia, and Singapore. Some even reached South Korea, Japan, and Australia.

Vietnamese refugees also crossed land borders, braving the horrors of the Khmer Rouge and Cambodia's killing fields in an attempt to find safety in Thailand. They also took great risks in crossing the Mekong River from Communist Laos to Thailand. Many perished in these land journeys.

Unbelievable Suffering of Boat Refugees

The stories of refugee suffering defy belief. From 1976–1983 I directed ministries in Southeast Asia for refugees that had fled Vietnam, Cambodia, and Laos. In my many personal encounters and from my Vietnamese-speaking staff dealing with Vietnamese boat refugees in five countries, I heard far too many horror stories.

A colleague in the Philippines ministered to a young Vietnamese girl who had been rescued from an atoll in the South China Sea by the Philippines navy. Her emaciated body bore the marks of the sharp beaks of seabirds that had started to feed on her. She herself had survived by cannibalizing her dead brother, the second-to-last survivor in a small boat whose engine had broken down, forcing it to drift for weeks.

One young boat refugee described to me how, in desperation, when he saw a fishing boat bearing down on his small craft, he had rubbed his wife's hair, face, and arms with dirty engine grease to make her unattractive to the Thai fishermen-cum-pirates. If refugees in a boat did not yield enough treasure in gold, jewelry, or money to the pirates' satisfaction, young women and girls were taken, sexually abused, and then often dumped into the sea to perish. Sometimes all girls and young women were made to strip naked on their boat so that the pirates could select the most attractive. Woe to any refugee husband, brother, or other man who dared defend the women aboard! Some of the attackers were Malaysian sailors. Refugees duly noted the official vessel numbers, but rarely was action taken (Mooneyham 1980).

I once assisted George Hoffman, founder of Tearfund UK, to interview a young Vietnamese woman, about twenty years of age. She had been taken from a refugee boat by pirates, incessantly raped and over several weeks passed among twenty-six different pirate boats for the same evil purpose! She was finally dropped overboard in the dead of night with a life buoy near the shore in southern Thailand by a pirate-fisherman she described as "one who had compassion on me." After making her way to shore, police arrested and imprisoned her because she was an alien trespasser without identification. I am not ashamed to say that such stories made me weep from deep sadness, sheer frustration, and hot rage.

World Vision sponsored a ship called *Seasweep* that tried to rescue refugees in distress at sea. Food for the Hungry supported a smaller ship, *The Akuna,* which they renamed *The Bamboo Cross.* Other commercial or navy ships encountering refugees in distress sometimes rescued them but often just sailed away from the inevitable "complications" involved in stopping to help. Many refugee boats saw no one on the vast expanse of the 250,000 square miles of the South China Sea.

Some would-be refugees' woes began even before they left Vietnam. It was common for unscrupulous boat organizers to defraud desperate people of huge sums of money with promises of safe passage which they never intended to keep, or even worse, to lead them into Communist police traps. Others were stopped by Vietnamese navy boats soon after embarking and returned to jails in Vietnam.

The large numbers of boat refugees severely tested the hospitality of the countries where they arrived. Sometimes boats were pushed back out to sea. Often refugees who made safe landfall were treated more as criminals than as victims of distress. In the end it was the international spotlight and the offer of assistance—from foreign governments and from private agencies, especially Christian ones—that forced or enabled some Southeast Asian countries to act humanely and allow their territory to be used as refugee way stations.

That hundreds of thousands of people, over nearly a decade, would knowingly take such huge risks is clear testimony to a very deep and widespread fear of life under communism.

Christian agencies such as World Relief US, Tearfund UK, the Salvation Army, World Vision, and Youth With A Mission were prominent among the many who responded to the needs of refugees in Southeast Asian refugee camps. Veteran Vietnamese-speaking missionaries often served with these agencies. Missionaries also helped organize refugee churches and build modest chapels in the camps. These often served as venues for evangelism and provided Christian contact and information for people who had much time on their hands! Thousands were led to the Christian faith through such ministries.

Organizations such as World Relief, related to the National Association of Evangelicals in the US, and the Mennonite Central Committee in Canada, became subcontractors for their respective governments in helping permanently resettle refugees in North America. In both the US and Canada, hundreds of churches were recruited to sponsor refugees. Through these processes, many Vietnamese were exposed to generous, caring Christians. Many placed their faith in Christ, and some joined the churches that had helped them. Many more joined Vietnamese-language churches related to the C&MA, the Southern Baptists, or the Mennonites, for example.

All along the lengthy and winding "refugee highway," refugees encountered caring Christians. As a result, many were attracted to the faith.

Not all refugees who became believers in Southeast Asian camps were able to resettle in third countries. They were "involuntarily" repatriated to Vietnam. But even in this, God was at work.

Some such as "Ms. Mai" became zealous evangelists once back in Vietnam (Voice of the Martyrs 2001, 259–92).

Guest Workers: Finding Christ in Communist Countries

The next wave of the Vietnamese diaspora involved many thousands of guest workers going abroad. In the 1980s Vietnam sent guest workers from the North to the Soviet Union and Eastern Bloc countries. Many returned home after the collapse of communism there.

During the uncertainty around the collapse of Soviet and Eastern European communism, Vietnamese Christians from North America and Europe went in small teams to those countries to share the gospel with Vietnamese workers. They worked through the network of the few Christians already there. They visited many workers in their dormitories, sharing the gospel and distributing gospel tracts. These efforts met with some success. Some became believers, and a number of cell groups were established. Today a significant number of house church leaders in northern Vietnam trace their conversion to their time in Russia, East Germany, and other former Communist countries.

One who traces his first contact with the gospel to East Germany is Nguyen Van Dai. When he returned to Vietnam he studied law and became a strong Christian believer. His vocation and his faith led him to activism for religious liberty, democracy, and human rights. In 2007 he was arrested for advocating by internet for a multiparty system and harming the state by exposing religious liberty abuses. He was released from Nam Ha prison on March 6, 2011 after serving a four-year sentence, but faces another four years of house arrest.

Lawyer Dai posted his conversion story on his blog shortly before his arrest. It is wonderfully illustrative of the way God uses the wanderings of Vietnamese around the world to bring them to Himself.

Why I Became a Believer in Jesus Christ

I worked in the former German Democratic Republic from November 1989 until October 1990. In July of 1990, after moving back and forth between the East and West Germanys became easier, a number of overseas Vietnamese Christians from various countries came to some cities in East Germany to share the gospel. A group of such young people came to the complex where I was living, talked to us, and distributed gospel tracts that explained about Jesus Christ. I had three roommates; all of us received some of those tracts. But at that time I was preparing to return to Vietnam. The factory in which I was working shut down, and we all had to scramble to find ways to make a little money before going back to Vietnam. So my friends and I did not have time to study the gospel tracts.

The day before returning home, we went out to look for an appropriate souvenir to take back to Vietnam. I looked long and hard but could not find anything I liked. Finally I spotted a small cross in a shop window. Although I did not know its meaning, I really liked it and decided to buy it. I hung the gold cross on a chain around my neck and went back to my quarters to pack my suitcase for the trip home. As I was packing, I again spotted the gospel tracts. I read some of them quickly and so began to have a little understanding of what the cross symbolized. I concluded I had chosen an item with great meaning.

Lawyer Nguyen Van Dai.

When I got back to Vietnam I entered university to study law. I became totally absorbed in my studies with no time to think much about the cross I had bought. My family followed Buddhism, so after graduating I would go to the Quan Su Pagoda on the first and fifteenth of the lunar month to worship and to pray for good things to happen to me. But through many months and years I never felt an inner peace, either in my life or in my work.

At the beginning of 2000, Mrs. Nguyen Thi Thuy, the leader of a house church in Viet Tri City, was arrested by the security police and sentenced by the people's court to a year in prison on the charge of "resisting an officer doing his duty." A group of international Christians in Hanoi gathered to pray about this situation and felt called to do something about this injustice by seeking a lawyer to defend her in the appeal court. They also shared their resources to help support Mrs. Thuy's family. Mrs. Thuy's family went to look for a lawyer to help them, but they were not successful.

One day a member of Mrs. Thuy's family went to the office of Lawyer Chau in the Trang Tri quarter of Hanoi. Lawyer Chau told them she would not take the case but would try to find someone who would. Eventually she came across my name and called me. She said she had a "sensitive case" and asked if I would take it. I replied that I would need to look at the file before deciding. So I went that afternoon to her office and read the three-page judgment of the people's court. I was shocked because I saw that the local authorities had illegally invaded the privacy of Mrs. Thuy's home, violated her freedom of religion, and arrested, tried, and imprisoned a person who was simply exercising her normal rights as a citizen. So I accepted the request to defend her.

As I researched her case to prepare for the appeal trial, I met many Christians who witnessed to me about the Lord Jesus and the cross. Then a foreign missionary came to visit me at my house. He told me that although he did not know Mrs. Thuy personally, he shared her faith. He added that when he heard that I was willing to defend her, he was very happy. Remarkably, not considering the great distance an obstacle, he came to Vietnam to seek me out. He told me that thousands of Christians all around the world were praying for the persecuted Mrs. Thuy and for me. When I heard these words, I was very moved. I remembered the cross I had purchased for myself a decade earlier. A few days later a friend invited me to an evangelistic meeting at the Protestant church at 2 Ngo Tram Street. On that occasion both my wife and I received the Lord Jesus Christ as our personal Savior. We are now Christian believers.

Lawyer Nguyen Van Dai, Hanoi, January 2007

(Note: Lawyer Dai was unsuccessful in his appeal for Mrs. Thuy, but his experience in defending her helped set his life on a new path.)

Exporting Labor and Importing the Gospel

In the first decade of the twenty-first century, a new wave of Vietnamese guest workers began to go to countries such as Malaysia, South Korea, and Taiwan, and some as far away as the Middle East. After completing one- or two-year contracts, they would return home. Vietnamese are industrious people by culture and desirable as workers. The number of this second wave of workers going abroad grew to be hundreds of thousands.

The majority of guest workers have gone to Malaysia. By 2009 more than 200,000 had been employed in that country, with about fifty-five thousand actively working. Mission organizations saw this as a great opportunity as northern Vietnam, where most of the first workers came from, had long been inaccessible to evangelism. So they recruited overseas Vietnamese and non-Vietnamese missionaries and even Vietnamese workers from Vietnam. Many Malaysian churches also joined in the efforts. Since 2002 a visionary

Malaysian lawyer has tirelessly promoted cooperation among the many organizations and people involved under the name of United Friendship Initiative (UFIN).

UFIN has reported that a full quarter of all guest workers who have gone to Malaysia have either attended Christian meetings, received Christian literature, or have been given social assistance by Christians. UFIN also provided legal advocacy help for workers. The majority of workers are sadly cheated or abused by their employers and the companies in Vietnam who recruit them. Extensive evangelistic activities among Vietnamese guest workers in Malaysia from 2003–2009 resulted in over twenty-seven thousand professions of faith. UFIN reports that about 20 percent of these have been successfully connected with churches in Vietnam when they return home.

In recent years northern ethnic minorities and some Montagnards have been included in guest workers going abroad. In 2009 about ten thousand of the fifty thousand guest workers from Vietnam in Malaysia were ethnic minorities. A few minority groups, totally unreached in Vietnam, had their first-ever encounter with the gospel there. Some became the first believers in their ethnic group while in Malaysia.

Ministries to guest workers from Vietnam are also taking place in South Korea. Some of the many Christian institutions in Korea are providing theological education to Vietnamese Christian leaders among the guest workers. In Taiwan one mission organization with a guest worker ministry added counseling for the many Vietnamese women who have married Taiwanese men in a bride-promotion scheme. The hope and promise of a better life for these women rarely materialized. They were often abused, and many tried to escape their unhappy marriages.

Vietnamese in Cambodia

A description of the Vietnamese diaspora must include Cambodia, where more than a million Vietnamese live. Many who went to Cambodia generations ago live on boats in floating villages in the Tonle Sap, eking out a living by fishing. The French also took skilled tradesmen from Vietnam to Cambodia during colonial times. Many very poor and uneducated Vietnamese today live in squalid slums in Phnom Penh and Siem Reap. Some Vietnamese soldiers and officials remained in Cambodia and brought their families after the Vietnam occupation of Cambodia ended in 1990. Thousands of

Vietnamese girls went to Cambodia to serve as prostitutes for the UN forces which had responsibility for Cambodia from 1991–1993. Many women never returned home. Even now an underworld network is recruiting more young girls in Vietnam.

Since the mid-1990s, a number of mission agencies and churches have initiated evangelism among Vietnamese in Cambodia. They responded in compassion, educating children without access to schools, ministering to victims of HIV/AIDS, and providing skills training, microloans, and other forms of assistance. However, in spite of this, evangelism efforts have struggled to plant stable and growing churches. Most workers who have attempted to evangelize Vietnamese in Cambodia say they have found them resistant to the gospel. In a survey in early 2010, Baptist missionary Paul Hai found a total of just over one thousand Christians in forty small congregations.

In summary we can see that Vietnamese who went abroad, whether under duress or voluntarily, often encountered Christians and the gospel. In unlikely circumstances many became Christian believers, and some returned to Vietnam to bless their country.

CHAPTER 10
Vietnam and Religious Freedom

Vietnam abandoned Marxist economics more than twenty years ago, improving the lives of millions of Vietnamese as a result. But, like the other four remaining Communist countries—North Korea, China, Laos, and Cuba—Vietnam has not abandoned its totalitarian, one-party system of government or its deep antipathy toward religion. Let's take a look at how Vietnam has dealt with religion, especially Protestantism, through its "laws," then assess the current situation and future prospects.

Open Doors' World Watch List, which ranks countries based on religious freedom from worst to better, has ranked Vietnam in the top-ten-worst category for eight of the last twelve years. The US State Department, which evaluates religious freedom in all countries it deals with, had Vietnam on its blacklist, called "Countries of Particular Concern" (CPC), from 2004–2006, along with fewer than ten other worst countries. These harsh rankings were well-deserved. Some recent improvement, though most welcome, does not mean all is well. Far from it.

Religion is considered an enemy of Communist revolutions, because it "drugs" oppressed people, keeping them from rising up, because they have hope of a better afterlife. According to orthodox communism, when the socialist system is working well, supplying people's material and social requirements, the need for religion will disappear. In practice, however, communism has not been content to let religion die on its own but has proactively tried to kill it.

History has proven that religion did not die under brutal Communist systems, either in the old Soviet Union or in the People's Republic of China. Indeed, heavy oppression sometimes seemed to make it flourish! This set up an ongoing conflict. Because of its persistence, religion must somehow be "temporarily" accommodated. The Communist system's only instinct is to control this persistent, dangerous, and threatening phenomenon called religion.

The first strategy is to co-opt leaders of a religion and harness them to the revolutionary cause. This is done by trying to create a "patriotic church" with leaders who are sympathetic to communism or at least malleable. As we have seen, Vietnamese authorities tried twice but failed to create a patriotic church out of the ECVN(S). They failed also in getting that church to reunite with the ECVN(N), which they did control for a time. But each such attempt stirred conflict between those who thought cooperation with the system would gain advantages and those who were resolutely convinced the other way.

Another control mechanism is the Fatherland Front (*Mat Tran To Quoc*), an instrument of the Party set up to be sure that "mass organizations" such as religious organizations, women's organizations, or labor unions, are on board and supporting the one official system. No organization under communism is allowed to be independent or to be a true voluntary, nongovernment organization. Having failed to co-opt the ECVN(S), the authorities' next strategy was to marginalize the church. They branded church leaders who would not cooperate with them as "bad people." For twenty-five years following the fall, most top leaders of the ECVN(S) respected by Christians were in the "bad people" category and were not allowed to function in their official roles. The church was not even allowed to hold its regular business meetings.

The "Law" and Religious Freedom

In Vietnam's 1992 constitution, Article 70 guarantees unqualified "freedom to believe or not to believe." It further states that "no one is allowed to infringe on this right." Vietnam is also a signatory to the Universal Declaration of Human Rights and the International Covenant of Civil and Political Rights. Both international agreements have clear clauses guaranteeing religious freedom. None of these commitments are honored by Vietnam in consistent, conforming practice.

Since reunification under communism, Vietnam has administered religion under a series of Religion Decrees. The last of these was Religion Decree 26 of 1999. Benefits and rights for religion were few and rarely honored. And worse, there were secret policies, especially directed at arresting the rapid growth of Christianity among Vietnam's ethnic minorities.

Vietnam maintains a large bureaucracy to oversee religion. There is a Government Bureau of Religious Affairs[23] with branches in many lower levels of government. There are special police units in the Ministry of Public Security assigned to monitor and control various religions.

Two Distinct and Conflicting Policies

When questioned about religious liberty shortcomings, Vietnam's authorities routinely point to their constitutional guarantee of religious freedom and other public documents ostensibly confirming the same. A whole other reality often exists out of public view.

In 2000, several government policy documents regarding Protestant Christianity, marked "secret" and "top secret," were acquired by religious freedom advocates, translated, and published under the title *Directions for Stopping Religion* (Freedom House Center for Religious Freedom 2000). These provided a rare window into the real attitudes and policies driving the repression of ethnic minority Protestants in Vietnam's Northwest Mountainous Region.

One of the documents expressed deep concern that Christian churches were instrumental in bringing down communism in Eastern Europe. Another document promoted ten policy recommendations to repress Christian churches, many of which are considered "hostile" and "dangerous." The same document includes the instructions to "work hard to control religious leaders" and "turn propaganda into an art form so they will not know they are being propagandized."

More sinister was the detailed description of a "Guidance Committee 184," made up of top officials at many levels to formulate and oversee the implementation of anti-Christian measures. Its mission was to "stop cold the contagious spread of the religion to the areas and minorities that do not yet have religion." The documents included a model form which Christians were to be "persuaded" to sign, indicating they were giving up their Christian beliefs and returning to their traditional animistic ones.

---

23 Often also translated as "Central Bureau of Religious Affairs" or "Committee of Religious Affairs"

In 2003 the Evangelical Fellowship of Canada Religious Liberty Commission published a paper entitled *Two Distinct and Conflicting Policies*.[24] It argued that it was not enough to coax Vietnam to do a little better by its public policies, but that Vietnam's internal, real policies needed to be challenged by democratic governments that valued human rights.

Surprising Recipients

Two Distinct and Conflicting Policies was distributed in high places that its authors had not anticipated. At that time a government religion official occasionally met with Vietnamese church leaders on a friendly basis. During a coffee discussion with one church leader, the official surprisingly pulled out a copy of this paper and asked the leader if he had seen it. The leader could honestly answer he had not, even though his insights had given the paper its name. The official said to him, "Regrettably for us this paper is mostly correct. I have put a copy of it on the desks of the top twenty-one leaders of our government." The official's staff had found the paper on a website of a French Catholic organization which had translated it into Vietnamese and posted it! It was an advocate's dream come true—the document was speaking truth to power.

An Advocacy Story

On June 30, 2004, six Vietnamese Mennonites were arrested four months after an altercation involving police who staked out the home (and office and church) of their leader, activist Pastor Nguyen Hong Quang. Included in the Mennonite Six, as they came to be known, was then twenty-one-year-old Ms. Le Thi Hong Lien. A bright and capable woman, she had been in charge of children's education for the church.

All six were imprisoned. The other five, all men, were allowed family visits beginning in August, but Ms. Lien was not allowed any until mid-October, three-and-a-half months after her arrest. By then her alarmed parents found their able and healthy daughter had become very ill and weak.

---

24 This and other documents on the religious freedom issue in Vietnam may be found at
    http://www.evangelicalfellowship.ca.

By the time of the November 12 trial, where each of the six was found guilty of "resisting an officer doing his duty," Ms. Lien was so weak that she could not stand up. Her pastor, also on trial, appealed to the judge that Lien was not physically fit to stand trial. He was told to shut up. Lien received a sentence of one year in prison. She was incarcerated first in the Chi Hoa Prison and later in the Tong Le Chan Prison.

When her parents were next allowed to visit her a few days after the trial, they were informed she had been taken to an outside hospital because she was seriously ill. When they next could visit, they were taken to see her in the prison infirmary. Her father reported that his daughter was so thin and weak that he could scarcely recognize her. She was covered with scabies and out of her mind. Her eyes were vacant. She did not recognize her parents, did not speak or respond, did not hear or understand what was going on around her, and cringed in fear at the mere shadow of a prison guard or official. Her arms and face were covered with bruises which her father surmised were from beatings. Along with physical abuse she had suffered a complete mental breakdown.

Lien's distraught father, Mr. Du, began telling the story of his daughter's pitiable situation widely, including to Radio Free Asia. As a result he was often denied the privilege of visiting Lien. When he was allowed to see her in mid-December, she looked even worse. Her left eye was black and swollen shut. She seemed quite unaware of what was going on around her.

A female prison guard told Mr. Du, "She has completely lost her mind and is filthy. She has no control over her bodily functions, defecating and urinating everywhere in her clothes." Her father felt certain that his daughter has been seriously abused and violated during her imprisonment, but feared complaining to officials might worsen her situation.

In February, the authorities transferred Ms. Lien to the Bien Hoa Mental Hospital where she remained until her release on April 28, two months short of her full sentence. Her release came only because of intense international advocacy— through prayer, government diplomacy, and advocacy organizations.

Ms. Lien with her father and friends on returning from her incarceration in the mental hospital.

One advocate was Emily, a foreign student in an international high school in Hanoi. She not only prayed diligently for Ms. Lien, but decided to help in other ways. She created an evocative three-dimensional piece of art (here pictured) with Ms. Lien in mind. She called it "Freedom." When Emily posted the art for sale on the internet to raise funds, I put in a bid and won. I later presented the "Freedom" piece to John Hanford III, then US Ambassador-at-Large for International Religious Freedom, in gratitude and memory of his significant part in securing the release of Ms. Lien and other prisoners.

Emily with her three-dimensional piece depicting raised hands holding bars.

The "New Religion Legislation"

Pressure to change began as Vietnam moved to join the free world's trading system. With the policy of "Doi Moi," or renovation, first announced in 1986, Vietnam steered sharply away from the Communist economic system toward a free market one. With that came international pressure for accountability in business, legal reforms, and other areas of economic activity.

Incentives and pressure to change increased markedly as Vietnam prepared to host the Asia-Pacific Economic Cooperation (APEC) in 2006. President George W. Bush had scheduled a state visit and Vietnam wanted badly to get off the CPC list in order to get Permanent Normal Trading Relations with the US, a prerequisite for joining the World Trade Organization.

Vietnam's draconian religion decrees, its repressive practices, and its failure to live up to the international agreements it had signed therefore came under more and more international scrutiny. Vietnam's response to this took some time, but in 2004–2005 Vietnam put forward three pieces of "new religion legislation" ostensibly intended to do better and satisfy international critics.

The Party laid the basis for change in a 2003 Communist Party Central Committee meeting. For the first time ever, it passed a resolution on religious activities. The official Party communiqué ominously said this action was designed "to increase state control over religious affairs." This Party resolution, which recognized that religion was still a need for some citizens, is cited as the basis for all subsequent legislation on religion.

In June 2004 an Ordinance on Belief and Religion, said to be a higher law than a decree, was published. It came into effect on November 15, 2004. In March 2005, Decree on Religion No. 22 was published for the purpose of explaining how to implement the Ordinance. And in February 2005, between the Ordinance and the Decree, the prime minister announced the unprecedented Special Directive No. 1 Concerning Protestants.[25]

The Ordinance contains six chapters with forty-one articles intended "to govern the activities of religious belief and religion." Decree on Religion No. 22 mirrors this with implementing instructions. These documents are noteworthy for their intrusiveness into all facets of religious life and organizations.

It was explained that the Ordinance improved on the earlier religion decrees, which were entirely based on the principle of "ask and receive." The Ordinance was said to simply require religious organizations to report

---

25 These and many other official as well as secret Vietnamese-language government documents on religion have been acquired by advocates, translated into English, and privately circulated for analysis.

approved activities. But in the experiences of Protestants there had been little observance of this difference.

The main advance of the new legislation was said to be a clear system of registration for churches so that they could become legal bodies. Curiously, one requirement for being considered for registration was "twenty years of stable operation." This meant an organization was required to operate il-legally for twenty years before it could be considered legal! Registration required two stages. The first was registration for a church organization "to carry on religious activities" wherever it had congregations. After another year of stable operation, an organization could be allowed to hold an orga-nizing general assembly, adopt a government-preapproved constitution for a four-year operating plan, and elect leaders.

Registration does not equal religious freedom, however. It does in theory offer official recognition, which is better than being considered illegal. But the government's purpose in giving registration to local churches or de-nominations is, by its own admission, to bring it "under management." It is therefore "religious freedom by management control." Denominations that have been granted full legal recognition have, in their words, "not found it convenient" to report most of their activities to the authorities. Some say they felt freer before registration. Nevertheless, the consensus is that it is best to take the limited legal legitimacy being offered in registration.

There was no way that officials countrywide could be expected to learn and implement this new registration system in time to show real progress in the fostering of religious freedom before the important events of 2006. So a "fire-extinguisher" solution was invented. This was the prime minister's Spe-cial Directive No. 1 Concerning the Protestant Religion of February 2005. This unprecedented directive for one religion was clearly a response to a lot of international advocacy on behalf of Vietnam's beleaguered Protestants. It directed commune- and city-level officials to provide prompt registration to individual house churches to carry on religious activities if they demonstrated a genuine need for religion.

The Directive included the oft-repeated warning against abusing religion for antigovernment purposes and, most significantly, the words, "Concerning the segment of society that follows the religion and now has a need to return to the traditional beliefs of their ethnic group, create favorable conditions and help them realize that desire." Sadly, it is this sentence which offers cover for forced recantations that officials have been more eager to implement than the directive to promptly register local churches.

US Ambassador-at-Large for International Religious Freedom, John Hanford III, hailed the new religion legislation as the greatest leap forward in religious freedom that he had ever seen in twenty years of advocacy work. Indeed, Vietnam did show early signs of good intentions to implement change. In 2005–2006 it registered a few hundred of the more than four thousand local Protestant congregations according to the prime minister's Special Directive. Vietnam promised the Americans it would move quickly to train its officials and get on with the rest of the registration project. It also promised an end to programs to force Christians to recant their faith. These promises were enough for Vietnam to be removed from the US CPC list on the eve of President Bush's participation in APEC and his state visit to Vietnam in 2006. Vietnam then also got US support to join the World Trade Organization early in 2007.

Having achieved its objectives, Vietnam soon began backsliding in its progress toward religious freedom and other human rights. Well after the new religion legislation of 2004–2005, authorities were still pursuing contrary secret programs to arrest or impede Christian growth. Researchers recently received secret 2007 government documents from Dien Bien in the Northwest Mountainous Region with testimonies from Christians there about the ongoing pressure on new believers to give up their faith. Only the name had changed. The dreaded "Guidance Committee 184," created in 1999 to suppress Christianity in the Northwest Provinces, now became "Guidance Committee 160."

Vietnam's Montagnards in the Central Highlands also remain under pressure, especially since their demonstrations against land confiscation and religious repression in 2001 and 2004. Following the April 2004 demonstrations, Vietnam reacted with major military operations against Montagnards in the Central Highlands, and then established the special Mobile Intervention Police unit (PA 43) which remains highly active to the present time.

Many, if not most, participants in these demonstrations were Christians, both Protestant and Catholic. But particular targets for retribution have been Dega Protestants, the organizers with connections to exiled members of an earlier independence movement. The Dega were accused of making the unacceptable demands that ethnic Vietnamese leave traditional Montagnard lands, and of wanting an independent country. In 2006, a "1,200 day campaign" was launched to eradicate Dega Protestantism.[26]

Part of the government's strategy is to pressure Dega Protestants to join the registered ECVN(S). This occurs without the ECVN(S)'s knowledge and consent and leads the Dega to call the ECVN(S) a compromised "government church," which it is not. This has caused serious tension between the groups, and of course, denies freedom of religious choice.

For some years the United Nations High Commission for Refugees (UNHCR) worked with Cambodia to provide safe havens to Montagnards fleeing Vietnam's crackdowns. But under Vietnam lobbying and pressure, the UNHCR and Cambodia agreed to abrogate that arrangement in February 2011. Now Montagnards, including Christians, who continue to suffer harassment, abuse, persecution, arrest, and imprisonment in their homeland have nowhere to flee.

Although the organizers of the these demonstrations include members of various tribes, they identified themselves as "Dega." This term, derived from the Ede-language phrase *anak ede gar,* means "children of the mountains." The Vietnam government has politicized Dega in the term *Tin Lanh Dega* (Dega Protestantism) which it deems an illegal subversive organization. Some exiled Montagnard groups self-identify as *Degar.* A demand or even a request by any group which seeks redress for injustice or minority rights is considered a dangerous political threat to the state.

It is not enough for Vietnam to point at improved "laws." The government must also create a culture of concern in which the laws are both understood as beneficial and will be enforced. So far Vietnam's Christians say their government "lacks sincerity" in this area.

"Peaceful Evolution"

Internal Party documents explain that the major threat to the Communist revolution is "peaceful evolution." The Communist Party believes that foreign enemies, especially the US, having lost the war of guns and bullets, have now changed tactics. The enemies' weapons of peaceful evolution are said to

---

26 For details on the government's campaigns against the Dega Protestants see Human Rights Watch March 2011 report, *Montagnard Christians in Vietnam: A Case Study in Religious Repression.*

be democracy, human rights, and religious freedom. And Protestants are the vanguard of this evolution in their quest for religious freedom.

This kind of thinking helps explain the serious and well-organized persecution that has been directed at the small Protestant minority for over a generation. Fortunately advocacy, international scrutiny, and political pressure have got Vietnam promising and saying some right things and making some improvements. Yet exceptions remain too frequent to be considered the actions of a few rogue officials, as Vietnam claims when pressed.

Vietnam has become more careful and subtle in its repression. Officials often arrange for new believers to be put under heavy family and community social pressure. This is intended to remove officials from the blunt edge of persecution. But officials in these situations are not hesitant to add and fulfill threats of physical abuse and loss of property. The combination of these two forces sometimes succeeds in making believers sign statements saying they have "voluntarily" given up their faith. As long as this goes on without consequences for participating officials, church leaders say they cannot trust the sincerity of the government's promises concerning religious freedom.

A Five-year Checkup

A five-year checkup of the new church registration policy should settle the question of whether the registration promises resulted in a great leap forward. It seems that it did not.

Two denominations, representing well over half of Vietnam's Christians, were actually granted full legal recognition before the new legislation: the ECVN(N) in the 1950s and the ECVN(S) in 2001. But this registration did not apply to the ethnic minority churches of their organizations. This meant that more than half of the ECVN(S) churches, those made up of ethnic minorities, needed to go through an additional, lengthy, government-supervised, church-by-church process. It is still not complete. As for the ECVN(N), only 160 of over one thousand ethnic minority congregations related to it had received provisional registration to carry on religious activities by the end of 2009. And even these congregations are not full members of the ECVN(N) as far as the government is concerned.

The prime minister's hurry-up-and-register-local-congregations directive has been a failure. After the initial spurt of such registration in 2005 and 2006, few registrations have been granted since. Most of the many hundreds of applications submitted have not even been given the courtesy of a reply, and some have been denied. Very few have been approved. In 2009, church leaders reported that not more than one tenth of house church applications for local registration submitted over the previous four years had been approved.

From 2007–2009 only seven of the seventy predominantly house church denominations completed the requirements for full legal recognition. One more, the Assemblies of God, has been allowed to begin the process. Contrary to the new legislation, it is the government, not the churches, that is responsible for initiating registration. If churches seek registration, they are told to wait. The majority of remaining unregistered groups do not meet the "twenty years of stable operation" requirement before registration can even be considered. Without denominational registration, or registration of local congregations, these groups remain vulnerable to arbitrary government harassment or worse.

Even at best, registration is not religious freedom. Vietnam says the purpose of registration is to bring churches under management control. Vietnam promises more legislation in the form of an ultimate "comprehensive law on religion." If there was real freedom, religious people and their organizations could easily be governed under common civil laws, as are all people in truly democratic jurisdictions worldwide.

In the words of one astute Protestant leader who must remain anonymous, "Our government pays far too much attention to us. As long as Vietnam makes special laws for religions, maintains a national religion bureaucracy, and assigns special police units to religions, it shows it highly suspects religion, and real religious freedom will not be possible."

"It Bends toward Justice"

However, our story has made quite clear that religious freedom as enjoyed in Western democracies is not necessary for Christians to flourish nor for churches to grow. Indeed, since Vietnam was united under communism thirty-five years ago, Protestant Christians there have multiplied nine times, sometimes under heavy persecution. For some, pressure and persecution has been a salutary experience. For many more it has made the choice to follow Jesus a very serious one, with the outcome often better than where the choice is more cost-free.

Martin Luther King Jr. once said, "The arc of the moral universe is long, but it bends toward justice." Ever so slowly Vietnam is being forced by internal and external forces to move in that direction. But as long as the ruling ideology retains both its disdain for and fear of the transcendent, Christians will be suspect and unjustly discriminated against. Our Creator and Redeemer is not pleased when His children are mistreated.

As a nation Vietnam hurts itself by marginalizing its potentially best citizens—Christians, who because of their beliefs, cherish and are willing to help the marginalized, the poor, and the sick. I have heard great pain expressed by leaders, who have nothing but good in mind for their nation and its people, at being persecuted and discriminated against. One prominent Christian leader who cares deeply for Vietnam was for two decades denied an ID card and passport. He remarked, "For twenty years my own country treated me like I did not exist, a nobody! I found that very painful." And heavier yet, some ethnic minority Christians, even in recent times, have been so cruelly persecuted that they felt no choice but to flee home, hearth, and land to seek freedom.

For Vietnam's churches, internal issues are often as great a concern as external restrictions. But the dynamism and grit of Vietnam's people, so clearly demonstrated everywhere in the Vietnam diaspora, is also regularly at work in individual Christian lives and in their churches at home. Add to that the power of God! The church will continue to *pha rao* (break fences) to grow and to leaven Vietnamese society as Vietnamese believers seamlessly speak and demonstrate the good news of Jesus Christ.

Nothing will stop it. Secret Vietnam government documents admit the same (Freedom House Center for Religious Freedom 2000). "The more we press, the faster it spreads and grows," they say.

Vietnamese Protestant churches not only continue to grow, but the day is already here when Vietnamese Christians are joining the wider Christian mission to take the gospel to the whole world!

References

Bao, N. (1994). *The sorrow of war*. London: Minerva.

Cadiere, L. (1929). *Religious Annamites et non Annamites* [Annamese and non-Annamese religions]. Trans. L. Greene. Paris: Un Empire Colonial Francaise, L'Indochine.

———. (1958). *Croyances et practiques religieuses des Vietnamiens* [Religious beliefs and practices of the Vietnamese]. 3 vols. Paris: Ecole Francaise d'Extreme-Orient.

Cadman, G. H. (1920). *Pen pictures of Annam and its people*. New York: Christian Alliance Press.

Central Population and Housing Census Steering Committee. (2010). *Report on completed census results: The 1/4/2009 population and housing census*. Hanoi: TDTDSVNO.

Chong, D. (1999). *The girl in the picture*. Toronto: Viking Press.

Cothonay, M. B. (1913). *Lives of twenty-six martyrs of Tonkin*. Dublin: Browne and Nolan.

Courtois, S., N. Werth, J. Panne, A. Paczkowski, K. Bartosek, and J. Margolin. (1999). *The black book of communism: Crimes, terror and repression*. Trans. J. Murphy and M. Kramer. Cambridge, MA: Harvard University Press.

Cowles, H. R. (1976). *Operation heartbeat*. Harrisburg, PA: Christian Publications.

de Rhodes, A. (1966). *Rhodes of Vietnam*. Trans. S. Hertz. Westminster, MD: The Newman Press. Originally published in France, 1651.

Doan, V. T. and Chanoff, D. (1986). *The Vietnamese gulag*. New York: Simon and Schuster.

Dowdy, H. E. (1964). *The bamboo cross: Christian witness in the jungles of Vietnam*. New York: Harper and Row.

Duiker, W. J. (2000). *Ho Chi Minh*. Crows Nest, NSW, Australia: Allen and Unwin.

Duong, T. H. (1993). *Paradise of the blind*. Trans. P. D. Duong and N. McPherson. New York: William Morrow.

———. (1995). *Novel without a name*. Trans. P. D. Duong and N. McPherson. New York: Penguin.

———. (2000). *Memories of a pure spring*. Trans. P. D. Duong and N. McPherson. New York: Penguin.

———. (2005). *No man's land: A novel*. Trans. P. D. Duong and N. McPherson. New York: Hyperion East.

Evangelical Fellowship of Canada Religious Liberty Commission. (2003). *Two Distinct and Conflicting Policies*. Ottawa: Evangelical Fellowship of Canada Religious Liberty Commission.

Freedom House Center for Religious Freedom. (2000). *Directions for stopping religion*. Washington, DC: Freedom House Center for Religious Freedom.

Gheddo, P. (1970). *The cross and the bo-tree: Catholics and Buddhists in Vietnam*. New York: Sheed and Ward.

Gobron, G. (1950). *History and philosophy of Caodaism*. Saigon: Tu-Hai Publishing House.

Government Bureau of Religious Affairs. (2008). *Training manual for the official management of the Protestant religion*. Hanoi.

Hayton, B. (2010a). *The limits to political activity in Vietnam*. East Asia Forum. http://www.eastasiaforum.org/2010/07/14/the-limits-to-political-activity-in-vietnam

———. (2010b). *Vietnam: Rising dragon*. New Haven, CT: Yale University Press.

Hefley, J. (1969). *By life or by death*. Grand Rapids, MI: Zondervan Publishing House.

Hefley, J. and M. Hefley. (1974). *No time for tombstones: Life and death in the Vietnamese jungle*. Wheaton, IL: Tyndale House Publishers.

———. (1976). *Prisoners of hope*. Harrisburg, PA: Christian Publications.

Hickey, G. C. (1982a). *Free in the forest: Ethnohistory of the Vietnamese Central Highlands from 1954 to 1976*. New Haven, CT: Yale University Press.

———. (1982b). *Sons of the mountains: Ethnohistory of the Vietnamese Central Highlands to 1954*. New Haven, CT: Yale University Press.

Hiebert, M. (1996). *Chasing the tigers: A portrait of the new Vietnam.* New York: Kodansha International.

Human Rights Watch. (2002). *Repression of Montagnards: Conflicts over land and religion in Vietnam's Central Highlands.* New York: Human Rights Watch.

———. (2011). *Montagnard Christians in Vietnam: A Case Study in Religious Repression.* New York: Human Rights Watch.

James, S. (2005). *Servants on the edge of history: Risking all for the gospel in war-ravaged Vietnam.* Garland, TX: Hannibal Books.

Jeffrey, D. I. (n.d.). Unpublished recollections of a pioneer missionary.

Jenkins, P. (2002). *The next Christendom: The rise of global Christianity.* New York: Oxford University Press.

———. (2006). *The new faces of Christianity: Believing the Bible in the Global South.* New York: Oxford University Press.

Lamb, D. (2002). *Vietnam now: A reporter returns.* New York: Public Affairs.

Le, H. P. (1972). A short history of the Evangelical Church of Vietnam. (Doctoral dissertation.) New York University.

Mandryk, J. (2010). *Operation World* (7th ed.). Colorado Springs, CO: Biblica Publishing.

Marx, K. and F. Engels. (1975). *Marx/Engels Collected Works.* New York: International Publishers.

McPherson, N. (n.d.) *An entry in the forthcoming "Encyclopedia on Southeast Asian literature."* http://www.vietnamlit.org/wiki/index.php?title=Duong_Thu_Huong

Miller, C. P. (1977). *Captured!* Chappaqua, NY: Christian Herald Books.

Mooneyham, W. S. (1980). *Sea of heartbreak.* Plainfield, NJ: Logos International.

Phan, P. C. (1998). *Mission and catechesis: Alexandre de Rhodes and inculturation in seventeenth-century Vietnam.* Maryknoll, NY: Orbis Books.

———. (2005). *Vietnamese-American Catholics.* New York/Mahwah, NJ: Paulist Press.

Pontifex, J. and J. Newton. (2011). "Persecuted and Forgotten? A Report on Christians Oppressed for their Faith." Sutton, UK: Aid to the Church in Need.

Reimer, R. E. (1972). The Protestant movement in Vietnam: Church growth in peace and war among ethnic Vietnamese. (Master's thesis). Fuller Theological Seminary, Pasadena, California.

————. (1974). *South Vietnam: Status of Christianity country profile*. Saigon: Office of Missionary Information. (Prepared for 1974 Lausanne Congress on World Evangelization).

Rohrer, N. B. (1984). *This poor man cried: The story of Larry Ward*. Wheaton, IL: Tyndale House Publishers.

Smith, G. H. (1942). *The blood hunters: A narrative of pioneer missionary work among the tribes of French Indo-China*. Chicago, IL: World Wide Prayer and Missionary Union.

————. (1947). *The missionary and primitive man*. Chicago, IL: Van Kampen Press.

Smith, L. I. (1943). *Gongs in the night: Reaching the tribes of French Indo-China*. Grand Rapids, MI: Zondervan Publishing House.

Steinkamp, O. N. (1973). *The Holy Spirit in Vietnam*. Carol Stream, IL: Creation House.

Templer, R. (1998). *Shadows and wind: A view of modern Vietnam*. London: Little Brown.

Tran, T. S. (1995). *Twenty years after*. Privately produced and circulated document.

Voice of the Martyrs. (2001). *Hearts of fire*. Nashville, TN: W Publishing Group.

Index